Fundamental Subjects: Content Knowledge Study Guide

▶ ▶ ▶ ▶ ▶ ▶ ▶ ▶ ▶ ▶ ▶

A PUBLICATION OF EDUCATIONAL TESTING SERVICE

Table of Contents

Study Guide for the *Fundamental Subjects: Content Knowledge* Test

► ► ► ► ► ► ► ► ► ► ► ►

TABLE OF CONTENTS

Chapter 1

Introduction to the *Fundamental Subjects: Content Knowledge* Test and
Suggestions for Using This Study Guide 1

Chapter 2

Background Information on The Praxis Series™ Assessments 7

Chapter 3

Succeeding on Multiple-Choice Questions 11

Chapter 4

Study Topics for the *Fundamental Subjects: Content Knowledge* Test 21

Chapter 5

Practice Questions for the *Fundamental Subjects: Content Knowledge* Test 69

Chapter 6

Right Answers and Explanations for the Practice Questions 107

Chapter 7

Are You Ready? Last-Minute Tips 125

Appendix A

Study Plan Sheet 129

Appendix B

For More Information 133

Chapter 1

**Introduction to the *Fundamental Subjects:
Content Knowledge* Test and Suggestions for
Using This Study Guide**

► ► ► ► ► ► ► ► ► ► ►

Introduction to the *Fundamental Subjects: Content Knowledge* Test

The Praxis *Fundamental Subjects: Content Knowledge* test assesses beginning teachers' understanding of general knowledge in the areas of English Language Arts, Mathematics, Citizenship and Social Science, and Science. In developing assessment material for this test, Educational Testing Service (ETS) works in collaboration with teacher educators, higher education content specialists, and accomplished practicing teachers to keep the test updated and representative of current standards.

The *Fundamental Subjects: Content Knowledge* test (0511) consists of 100 multiple-choice questions and covers four major areas, in the following proportions:

Content Category	Number of Questions	Percentage of Examination
English Language Arts	25	25
Mathematics	25	25
Citizenship and Social Science	25	25
Science	25	25

Test takers have two hours to complete the test.

Questions are arranged in the test book by subject. An index on the back page of the test book identifies the page locations where you can find each subject. You may answer the questions in any order you choose. You may use a nonprogrammable calculator while taking the test; a basic four-function calculator will be adequate.

How to Use This Study Guide

This study guide gives you instruction, practice, and test-taking tips to help you prepare for taking the *Fundamental Subjects: Content Knowledge* test. In chapter 2 you will find a description of The Praxis Series™—what it is and how the tests in The Praxis Series are developed. In chapter 3 you will find information on how to answer multiple-choice questions. Then chapters 4, 5, and 6 will help you prepare for the test, give you the chance to take a practice test, and provide you with explanations for the correct answers to the practice test questions.

Suggestions for Using the "Study Topics" Chapter

We recommend the following approach for using the "Study Topics" chapter to prepare for the test.

Become familiar with the test content. Learn what will be assessed in the test by reading chapter 4.

Assess how well you know the content in each area. After you learn what topics the test contains, you should assess your knowledge in each area. How well do you know the material? In which areas do you need to learn more before you take the test? It is quite likely that you will need to brush up on most or all of the areas.

Develop a study plan. Assess what you need to study and create a realistic plan for studying. You can develop your study plan in any way that works best for you. A "Study Plan" form is included in appendix A at the end of the book as a possible way to structure your planning. Remember that this is a licensure test and covers a great deal of material. Plan to review carefully. You will need to allow time to find the books and other materials, time to read the material and take notes, and time to go over your notes.

Identify study materials. The material covered by the test is at the level commonly covered in standard introductory textbooks. Books used in secondary classrooms may also prove useful to you, since they also present the material you need to know. If you do not own introductory texts that cover all the areas, you may want to borrow some from friends or from a library. You may also want to obtain a copy of your state's academic standards from the state's Department of Education Web site.

Use standard school and college introductory textbooks and other reliable, professionally prepared materials. Don't rely heavily on information provided by friends or from searching the World Wide Web. Neither of these sources is as uniformly reliable as textbooks.

Work through your study plan. You may want to work alone, or you may find it more helpful to work with a group or with a mentor. Work through the topics and questions provided in chapter 4. Rather than memorizing definitions from books, be able to define and discuss the topics in your own words and understand the relationships between diverse topics and concepts. If you are working with a group or mentor, you can also try informal quizzes and questioning techniques.

Proceed to the practice questions. Once you have completed your review, you are ready to benefit from the "Practice Questions" portion of this guide.

Suggestions for Using the "Practice Questions" and "Right Answers and Explanations" Chapters

Read chapter 3. This chapter will sharpen your skills in reading and answering multiple-choice questions. For you to succeed on multiple-choice questions, you must focus carefully on the question, avoid reading things into the question, pay attention to details, and sift patiently through the answer choices.

Take the practice test in chapter 5. Work on the practice questions in a quiet place without distractions. Remember that the practice questions are only examples of the way the topics are covered in the test. The test will have different questions.

Score the practice questions. Go through the detailed answers in chapter 6 ("Right Answers and Explanations"). Mark the questions you answered correctly, as well as the ones you missed. Look over the explanations of the questions you missed and see if you understand them.

Decide whether you need more review. After you have looked at your results, decide whether there are areas that you need to brush up on before taking the actual test. Go back to your textbooks and reference materials to see if the topics are covered there. You might also want to go over your questions with a friend or teacher who is familiar with the subjects.

Assess your readiness. Do you feel confident about your level of understanding in each of the areas? If not, where do you need more work? If you feel ready, complete the checklist in chapter 7 ("Are You Ready?") to double-check that you've thought through the details. If you need more information about registration or the testing situation itself, use the resources in appendix B: "For More Information."

Note: Every effort is made to provide the most recent information in this study guide. However, The Praxis Series tests are continually evaluated and updated. You will always find the most recent information about this test, including the topics covered, number of questions, and time allotted, in the *Test at a Glance* booklet available online at http://www.ets.org/praxis/prxtest.html.

Chapter 2
Background Information on The Praxis Series™ Assessments

▶   ▶   ▶   ▶   ▶   ▶   ▶   ▶   ▶   ▶   ▶   ▶

What Are The Praxis Series™ Subject Assessments?

The Praxis Series™ Subject Assessments are designed by Educational Testing Service (ETS) to assess your knowledge of subjects that are relevant to your teaching career, and they are a part of the licensing requirements in many states. This study guide, for example, covers an assessment that tests your general understanding of English Language Arts, Mathematics, Citizenship and Social Science, and Science. Your state has adopted this Praxis test because it wants to be certain that you have achieved a specified level of understanding in these subjects before it grants you a license to teach in a classroom.

The passing score for each test is set by the state. You can find the passing scores online at www.ets.org/praxis/prxstate.html or in the *Understanding Your Praxis Scores* pamphlet, available in your college's School of Education or by calling ETS at 609-771-7395 or 800-772-9476.

What Is Licensure?

Licensure in any area—medicine, law, architecture, accounting, cosmetology—is an assurance to the public that the person holding the license possesses sufficient knowledge and skills to perform important occupational activities safely and effectively. In the case of teacher licensing, a license tells the public that the person holding the license can be trusted to educate children competently and professionally.

Because a license makes such a serious claim about its holder, licensure requirements can be quite demanding. In some fields licensure tests have more than one part and last for more than one day. Candidates for licensure in all fields plan intensive study as part of their professional preparation: some join study groups, others study alone. But preparing to take a licensure test is, in all cases, a professional activity. Preparing for a licensure exam takes planning, discipline, and sustained effort. Studying thoroughly is highly recommended.

Why Does My State Require The Praxis Series Assessments?

Your state chose The Praxis Series Assessments because the tests assess the breadth and depth of content—called the "domain"—that your state wants its teachers to possess before they begin to teach. The level of knowledge, reflected in each test's passing score, is based on recommendations of panels of teachers and teacher educators in each subject area. The state licensing agency and, in some states, the state legislature ratify the passing scores that have been recommended by panels of teachers.

What Kinds of Tests Are The Praxis Series Subject Assessments?

Two kinds of tests comprise The Praxis Series Subject Assessments: multiple-choice (for which you select your answer from a list of choices) and constructed-response (for which you write a response of your own). Multiple-choice tests can measure a wider area of content knowledge because they can ask more questions in a limited period of time. Constructed-response tests have fewer questions, but the questions require you to demonstrate the depth of your knowledge in the area covered.

How Were These Tests Developed?

ETS began the development of The Praxis Series Subject Assessments with a survey. For each subject, teachers around the country in various teaching situations were asked to judge what knowledge and skills a beginning teacher needs to possess. Professors in schools of education who prepare teachers were asked the same questions. These responses were ranked in order of importance and sent out to hundreds of teachers for review. All of the responses to these surveys (called "job analysis surveys") were analyzed to summarize the judgments of these professionals. From their consensus, ETS developed the specifications (guidelines) for the multiple-choice and constructed-response tests. Each subject area had a committee of practicing teachers and teacher educators who wrote the specifications, which were reviewed and eventually approved by teachers. From the test specifications, groups of teachers and professional test developers created test questions.

When your state adopted The Praxis Series Subject Assessments, local panels of practicing teachers and teacher educators in each subject area met to examine each test and to evaluate its relevance to beginning teachers in your state. This is called a "validity study" because local practicing professionals validate that the test content is relevant to the job. During the validity study, the panel also provides a passing-score recommendation. This process includes a rigorous review to determine how many test questions a beginning teacher in that state would be able to answer correctly. The state or licensing agency then reviewed the study recommendations and made a final determination of the passing-score requirement.

Throughout the development process, practitioners in the teaching field—teachers and teacher educators—participated in defining what the tests would cover, which tests would be used for licensure, and what score(s) would be needed to achieve licensure. This practice is consistent with how licensure works in most fields: those who are already licensed oversee the licensing of new practitioners. When you pass The Praxis Series Subject Assessments, you and the practitioners in your state will have evidence that you have the knowledge required to begin practicing your profession.

Chapter 3
Succeeding on Multiple-Choice Questions

▶ ▶ ▶ ▶ ▶ ▶ ▶ ▶ ▶ ▶ ▶ ▶

Understanding Multiple-Choice Questions

When you read multiple-choice questions on the Praxis *Fundamental Subjects: Content Knowledge* test, you will probably notice that many test questions contain the phrase "which of the following."

In order to answer a multiple-choice question successfully, you need to consider carefully the context set up by the question and limit your choice of answers to the list given. The purpose of the phrase "which of the following" is to remind you to do this. For example, look at this question.

Which of the following is a flavor made from beans?

(A)   Strawberry
(B)   Cherry
(C)   Vanilla
(D)   Mint

You may know that chocolate and coffee are also flavors made from beans, but they are not listed, and the question asks you to select from the list that follows ("which of the following"). So the answer has to be the only bean-derived flavor in the list: vanilla.

Notice that the answer can be substituted for the phrase "which of the following." In the question above, you could insert "vanilla" for "which of the following" and have the sentence "Vanilla is a flavor made from beans." Sometimes it helps to cross out "which of the following" and insert the various choices. You may want to give this technique a try as you answer various multiple-choice questions on the practice test.

Looking carefully at the "which of the following" phrase helps you to focus on what the question is asking you to find and on the answer choices. In the simple example above, all of the answer choices are flavors. Your job is to decide which of the flavors is the one made from beans.

The vanilla bean question is pretty straightforward. But the phrase "which of the following" can also be found in more challenging questions. Look at this question:

Which of the following is an effect of inflation?

(A)   Consumer buying power decreases.
(B)   Consumer buying power increases.
(C)   Interest rates generally decline.
(D)   Exports increase.

The placement of "which of the following" tells you that the choices are a list of possible effects (in this case, these are possible effects of inflation). What are you supposed to find as an answer? You are supposed to find the choice that most clearly illustrates the impact of inflation.

Educational Testing Service (ETS) question writers and editors work very hard to word each question as clearly as possible. Sometimes, though, it helps to put the question in your own words. Here, you could paraphrase the question, as "People would feel inflation in which of the following ways?" The correct answer is (A). (Inflation is an economic condition characterized by a general rise in prices throughout an economy. In periods of high inflation, the same amount of money buys far fewer goods; therefore, consumer buying power, in general, decreases.)

You may also find that it helps you to circle or underline each of the critical details of the question in your test book so that you don't miss any of them. It's only by looking at all parts of the question carefully that you will have all of the information you need to answer it. Circle or underline the critical parts of what is being asked in this question:

Homeostasis in a living organism is regulated by feedback. This process is most similar to which of the following?

(A) An electric light switch
(B) An escalator between floors of a store
(C) The thermostat on a central heating system
(D) The gas pedal on an automobile

Here is one possible way you may have annotated the question:

Homeostasis in a living organism is regulated by feedback. This process is most similar to which of the following?

(A) An electric light switch
(B) An escalator between floors of a store
(C) The thermostat on a central heating system
(D) The gas pedal on an automobile

After thinking about the question, you can probably see that you are being asked to look at a list of choices that represent possible analogies to homeostasis. The correct answer is (C). The important thing is understanding what the question is asking. With enough practice, you should be able to determine what any question is asking. Knowing the answer is, of course, a different matter, but you have to understand a question before you can answer it correctly.

Understanding Questions Containing "NOT," "LEAST," or "EXCEPT"

The words "NOT," "LEAST," and "EXCEPT" can make comprehension of test questions more difficult. They ask you to select the choice that *doesn't* fit. You must be very careful with this question type because it's easy to forget that you're selecting the negative. This question type is used in situations in which there are several good solutions, or ways to approach something, but also a clearly wrong way. These words are always capitalized when they appear in The Praxis Series test questions, but they are easily (and frequently) overlooked.

For the following test question, determine what kind of answer you need and what the details of the question are:

> During the nineteenth century, some bird species, such as starlings, were introduced into the United States from Europe. Since then they have spread throughout the country and become a nuisance, or pest species, especially in urban areas. They often drive native birds out of their habitats. Factors that have contributed to the starling's success in the United States most likely include all of the following EXCEPT
>
> (A) appropriate locations for nesting
> (B) suitable range of temperatures
> (C) an abundance of natural predators
> (D) availability of a variety of food sources

You are looking for a factor that would NOT explain the success of the starling in its spread throughout the United States. (C) is the correct answer—all of the other choices *are* factors that help to explain the spread of the starling.

TIP

It's easy to get confused while you're processing the information to answer a question with a NOT, LEAST, or EXCEPT in the question. If you treat the word "NOT," "LEAST," or "EXCEPT" as one of the details you must satisfy, you have a better chance of understanding what the question is asking.

Be Familiar with Multiple-Choice Question Types

You will probably see more than one question format on a multiple-choice test. Here are examples of some of the more common question formats.

1. Complete the statement

In this type of question, you are given an incomplete statement. You must select the choice that will make the completed statement correct.

The following excerpt is from a speech by William Safire.

Is the decline of the written word inevitable? Will the historians of the future deal merely in oral history? I hope not. I hope that oral history will limit itself to the discovery of toothpaste and the invention of mouthwash. I don't want to witness the decomposing of the art of composition, or be present when we get in touch with our feelings and lose contact with our minds.

It can be inferred from the passage that the author believes that, in contrast to oral history, the written word is

(A) able to convey emotions more accurately
(B) a more intellectual exercise
(C) doomed to describe mundane historical events
(D) already obsolete

To check your answer, reread the question and add your answer choice at the end. Be sure that your choice best completes the sentence. The correct answer is (B).

2. Which of the following

This question type is discussed in detail in a previous section. The question contains the details that must be satisfied for a correct answer, and it uses "which of the following" to limit the choices to the four choices shown, as this example demonstrates. In contrast to the earlier example, the phrase "which of the following" here comes at the end of the question. The placement of this phrase does not change the way you should approach the question.

According to the United States Constitution, the President is given the power to do which of the following?

(A) Impeach judges
(B) Pass laws
(C) Coin money
(D) Veto bills

The correct answer is (D).

3. Roman numeral choices

This format is used when there can be more than one correct answer in the list. Consider the following example:

For the greater part of the time humankind has existed on Earth, people have obtained their food by which of the following means?

  I. Hunting
 II. Gathering
III. Agriculture

(A) I only
(B) III only
(C) I and II only
(D) I and III only

One useful strategy for this type of question is to assess each possible answer before looking at the answer choices and then evaluate the answer choices. The oldest known remains of *homo sapiens* have been dated at 75,000 to 115,000 years old. The earliest evidence from agriculture dates from 10,000 years ago. Until then, humans survived only by hunting animals and gathering plants for food. Therefore, the correct answer is (C).

4. Questions containing NOT, LEAST, EXCEPT

This question type is discussed at length above. It asks you to select the choice that doesn't fit.

5. Questions about graphs or tables

The important thing to keep in mind when answering questions about tables, graphs, or reading passages is to answer the question that is asked. In the case of a map or graph, you should consider reading the question first, and then look at the map or graph in light of the question(s) you have to answer.

Look at this example.

BUDGET FOR SCHOOL TRIP

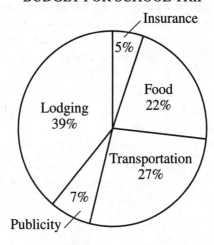

Total Budget: $12,000

How much money was budgeted for transportation for the school trip?

(A) $2,700
(B) $2,810
(C) $3,060
(D) $3,240

There is no reason to spend a great deal of time trying to understand the entire graph in detail when you are being asked a very specific question about it. Here the best approach is to read the question and then look at the graph with the question in mind. You can quickly see the total amount budgeted for the school trip is $12,000 and the percent of the total budget allocated to transportation is 27%. By expressing 27% as a decimal 0.27 and multiplying $12,000 by that decimal

$$0.27 \times \$12,000 = \$3,240$$

you find the amount budgeted for transportation, so the answer is (D).

Here is another example.

RECORD LOW TEMPERATURES AT TANNERSVILLE, PA	
Month	Record Low (degrees Fahrenheit)
January	–31
February	–25
March	–14
April	11
May	22
June	31
July	39
August	32
September	22
October	12
November	–6
December	–19

The monthly low temperatures in degrees Fahrenheit for Tannersville, Pennsylvania, are given in the table above. What is the range of the record low temperatures for Tannersville?
(The range is the difference between the highest and the lowest number in a set of values.)

(A)   8
(B)   12
(C)   62
(D)   70

As with the question about the graph on the previous page, the best way to approach this question would be to look at the question before studying the table. You might, however, want to look over the table briefly in order to get yourself oriented. (What is it about? How is it organized?) But the key to answering correctly is reading the question and using the table to answer it.

The question provides you with a definition of *range* to apply when using the table. You need to locate the lowest record low temperature, in degrees Fahrenheit (–31) and the highest record low temperature (39). Using the definition given, subtract –31 from 39:

$$39 - (-31) = 70$$

Thus, the range is 70 degrees. The correct answer is (D).

6. Other formats

New formats are developed from time to time in order to find new ways of assessing knowledge with multiple-choice questions. If you see a format you are not familiar with, read the directions carefully. Then read and approach the question the way you would any other question, asking yourself what you are supposed to be looking for and what details are given in the question that help you find the answer.

Other Useful Facts About the Test

1. **You can answer the questions in any order.** You can go through the questions from beginning to end, as many test takers do, or you can create your own path. Perhaps you will want to answer questions in your strongest area of knowledge first and then move from your strengths to your weaker areas. There is no right or wrong way. Use the approach that works best for you.

2. **There are no trick questions on the test.** You don't have to find any hidden meanings or worry about trick wording. All of the questions on the test ask about subject matter knowledge in a straightforward manner.

3. **Don't worry about answer patterns.** There is one myth that says that answers on multiple-choice tests follow patterns. There is another myth that there will never be more than two questions with the same lettered answer following each other. There is no truth to either of these myths. Select the answer you think is correct based on your knowledge of the subject.

4. **There is no penalty for guessing.** Your test score for multiple-choice questions is based on the number of correct answers you have. When you don't know the answer to a question, try to eliminate any obviously wrong answers and then guess at the correct one.

5. **It's OK to write in your test booklet.** You can work out problems right on the pages of the booklet, make notes to yourself, mark questions you want to review later, or write anything at all. Your test booklet will be destroyed after you are finished with it, so use it in any way that is helpful to you. But make sure to mark your answers on the answer sheet.

Smart Tips for Taking the Test

1. **Put your answers in the right "bubbles."** It seems obvious, but be sure that you are filling in the answer "bubble" that corresponds to the question you are answering. A significant number of test takers fill in a bubble without checking to see that the number matches the question they are answering.

2. **Skip the questions you find extremely difficult.** There are sure to be some questions that you think are hard. Rather than trying to answer these on your first pass through the test, leave them blank and mark them in your test booklet so that you can come back to them later. Pay attention to the time as you answer the rest of the questions on the test, and try to finish with 10 or 15 minutes remaining so that you can go back over the questions you left blank. Even if you don't know the answer the second time you read the questions, see whether you can narrow down the possible answers, and then guess.

3. **Keep track of the time.** Bring a watch to the test, just in case the clock in the test room is difficult for you to see. You will probably have plenty of time to answer all of the questions, but if you find yourself becoming bogged down in one section, you might decide to move on and come back to that section later.

4. **Read all of the possible answers before selecting one**—and then reread the question to be sure the answer you have selected really answers the question being asked. Remember that a question that contains a phrase such as "Which of the following does NOT..." is asking for the one answer that is NOT a correct statement or conclusion.

5. **Check your answers.** If you have extra time left over at the end of the test, look over each question and make sure that you have filled in the "bubble" on the answer sheet as you intended. Many test takers make careless mistakes that they could have corrected if they had checked their answers.

6. **Don't worry about your score when you are taking the test.** No one is expected to answer all of the questions correctly. Your score on this test is *not* analogous to your score on the SAT, the GRE, or other similar-looking (but in fact very different!) tests. It doesn't matter on this test whether you score very high or barely pass. If you meet the minimum passing scores for your state and you meet the state's other requirements for obtaining a teaching license, you will receive a license. In other words, your actual score doesn't matter, as long as it is above the minimum required score. With your score report you will receive a booklet entitled *Understanding Your Praxis Scores*, which lists the passing scores for your state.

Chapter 4

Study Topics for the *Fundamental Subjects: Content Knowledge* Test

▶   ▶   ▶   ▶   ▶   ▶   ▶   ▶   ▶   ▶   ▶   ▶

Introduction to the Test

The *Fundamental Subjects: Content Knowledge* test (0511) consists of 100 multiple-choice questions and covers four major areas, in the following proportions:

Content Category	Number of Questions	Percentage of Examination
English Language Arts	25	25
Mathematics	25	25
Citizenship and Social Science	25	25
Science	25	25

Test takers have two hours to complete the test.

Questions are arranged in the test book by subject. An index on the back page of the test book identifies the page locations where you can find each subject. You may answer the questions in any order you choose. You may use a nonprogrammable calculator while taking the test; a basic four-function calculator will be adequate.

The test is not intended to assess teaching skills, nor is it predicated on the assumption that you should be an expert in all of the subjects. Since the examination's purpose is to assess knowledge and skills in subject matter that may lie outside your teaching specialization, the questions in each subject focus on key indicators of general knowledge and understanding, requiring you to utilize fundamental skills that are founded upon broad concepts in each of the subjects.

This chapter is intended to help you organize your preparation for the test and to give you a clear indication of the depth and breadth of the knowledge required for success on the test.

Using the topic lists that follow: You are not expected to be an expert on all aspects of the topics that follow. You should understand the major characteristics of each topic and have some familiarity with the subtopics. You are likely to find that the topics are covered by most introductory textbooks in the subject areas. Try not to be overwhelmed by the volume and scope of knowledge and skills in this guide. Although a specific term may not seem familiar as you see it here, you might find you can understand it when it is applied to a real-life situation. Many of the questions on the actual Praxis test will provide you with a context in which to apply these topics or terms, as you will see when you look at the practice questions in chapter 5.

Special questions marked with stars: Interspersed throughout the list of topics are questions that are outlined in boxes and preceded by stars (★). These questions show how you might pay attention to particular concepts in preparing for the test. If you spend time on these questions, you will likely gain increased understanding and a facility with the subject matter covered on the test. You may want to discuss with a teacher, mentor, or colleague the questions outlined in the boxes and your answers.

Note that the questions outlined in the boxes are in general open-ended questions, not multiple-choice questions. They are intended as *study* questions, not practice questions. Thinking about the answers to the open-ended questions will improve your understanding of fundamental concepts and is likely to help you answer a number of related multiple-choice questions. For example, consider the following question that appears under the mathematics topic "Apply place value concepts and numeration to ordering and grouping."

★   To find the time, in hours, that has elapsed from 11:45 A.M. to 6:25 P.M. on the same day, could either of the following computations be used to find the answer? Why or why not?

$$11.45 \qquad\qquad 18\frac{5}{12}$$
$$\underline{-\ 6.25} \qquad\qquad \underline{-11\frac{3}{4}}$$

If you answer and think about this question, then you have probably prepared yourself to answer the following multiple-choice question.

A machine began processing a production order at 10:20 A.M. and by 2:55 P.M. the machine had completed $\frac{5}{6}$ of the order. If the machine processed the order yesterday nonstop and at a constant rate, at what time did the machine finish?

(A)   3:20 P.M.
(B)   3:50 P.M.
(C)   4:15 P.M.
(D)   4:30 P.M.

The correct answer is (B).

Study Topics: English Language Arts

The English Language Arts section of the *Fundamental Subjects: Content Knowledge* test covers interpretation of literature, understanding the effects created by literary elements, reading comprehension, and issues in writing and speaking.

Here is an overview of the areas covered in the "English Language Arts" section:

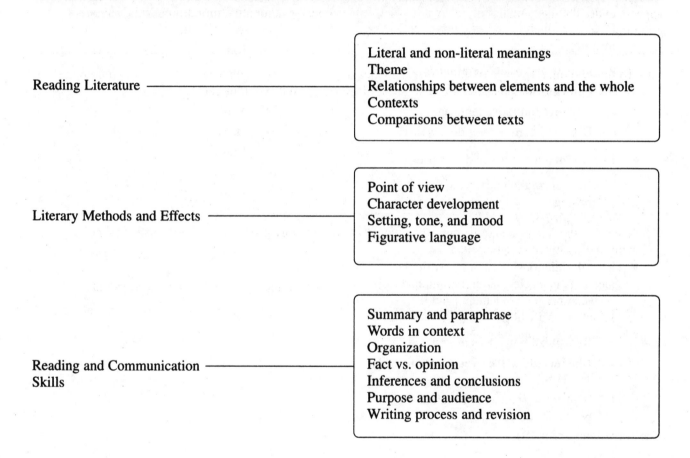

Reading Literature

- Literal and non-literal meanings
- Theme
- Relationships between elements and the whole
- Contexts
- Comparisons between texts

Literary Methods and Effects

- Point of view
- Character development
- Setting, tone, and mood
- Figurative language

Reading and Communication Skills

- Summary and paraphrase
- Words in context
- Organization
- Fact vs. opinion
- Inferences and conclusions
- Purpose and audience
- Writing process and revision

Reading Literature

This part of the test emphasizes comprehension, interpretation, and analysis of literary works. No previous experience with the supplied passages is required.

Understand and interpret literary texts

- Recognize literal and basic non-literal meanings
  - ▶ Understand basic literal meanings
  - ▶ Understand implications
  - ▶ Interpret figurative language
  - ▶ Distinguish important details

- Identify major themes and purposes
  - ▶ Recognize the underlying theme of a passage
  - ▶ Identify the details of a passage that contribute to the theme of the passage

- Identify relationships among particular elements in a selection and relationships between particular elements and the selection as a whole
  - ▶ Recognize how ideas are related
  - ▶ Link details to the overall meaning of the text
  - ▶ Identify why an author includes a particular detail

- Understand literary texts in their historical, cultural, and cross-cultural contexts
  - ▶ Identify features of a text that concern social and cultural issues
  - ▶ Consider how issues related to gender, race, history, and class are presented in a text

- Make comparisons among literary texts
  - ▶ Identify similarities and differences between selections
    - ◆ Tone
    - ◆ Imagery
    - ◆ Purpose
    - ◆ Audience
    - ◆ Ideas
    - ◆ Theme

Literary Methods and Effects

This part of the test emphasizes interpretation of literary elements. You will not be required to demonstrate knowledge of specialized literary vocabulary.

Understand the meanings and effects created by specific literary elements

- Identify the point of view of the selection and recognize how words and phrases in the selection indicate that point of view

  ▶ Recognize who is speaking

  ▶ Identify the characteristics of the speaker

- Identify aspects of specific characters and recognize how words and phrases in the selection contribute to their development

  ▶ Characterization through details (clothing, physical appearance, etc.)

  ▶ Characterization through actions and interactions with others

  ▶ Characterization through description (e.g., adjectives)

- Recognize the setting, tone, and mood of the selection and how words and phrases in the selection contribute to their development

  ▶ Temporal setting

  ▶ Physical setting

  ▶ Narrative tone (e.g., optimistic, melancholy, enthusiastic, regretful)

    ◆ Developed through description

    ◆ Developed through details of scenery, behavior, etc.

- Recognize the meanings and effects created through the use of imagery and figurative language. You may encounter literary devices such as metaphor, simile, and foreshadowing. While you will not have to identify these devices by name, you should be able to understand how they function within a text.

Exercise Related to the "Understand and interpret literary texts" and "Understand the meanings and effects created by specific literary elements" Topics

The following exercise and annotated sample are intended to give you practice in the kind of interpretive thinking about literature that is expected in the sections of the test described on the previous pages. Although the format of this annotation exercise is not like that of the multiple-choice questions on the test, the skills of interpretation and evaluation needed to complete it are comparable. For this exercise, read the poem and questions and try to annotate the poem in response to the questions. Then, read the annotated version on the following page and compare your analysis.

★ *Read the following poem, E. B. White's "Natural History."*
What is the point of view of the poem? What is its tone?
What kinds of figurative language does it use?

The spider, dropping down from twig,
Unwinds a thread of her devising:
A thin, premeditated rig
To use in rising.

And all the journey down through space,
In cool descent, and loyal-hearted,
She builds a ladder to the place
From which she started.

Thus I, gone forth, as spiders do,
In spider's web a truth discerning,
Attach one silken strand to you
For my returning.

All lines from "NATURAL HISTORY" from POEMS AND SKETCHES OF
E. B. WHITE by E. B. White. Copyright 1929 by E. B. White. Reprinted by
permission of HarperCollins Publishing Inc.

Here is the same poem with annotations that relate to the questions on the previous page.

The spider, dropping down from twig,
Unwinds a thread of her devising:
A thin, premeditated rig
To use in rising.

And all the journey down through space,
In cool descent, and loyal-hearted,
She builds a ladder to the place
From which she started.

Thus I, gone forth, as spiders do,
In spider's web a truth discerning,
Attach one silken strand to you
For my returning.

All lines from "NATURAL HISTORY" from POEMS AND SKETCHES OF E. B. WHITE by E. B. White. Copyright 1929 by E. B. White. Reprinted by permission of HarperCollins Publishing Inc.

The poem compares the spider's web to a climbing rig and a ladder.

The use of "I" signals for the first time in the poem that there is a speaker observing the spider.

The spider is portrayed through human-like actions.

The speaker compares himself to spiders (comparison is signaled by the word "as").

The final two lines reveal that the poem is addressed to a lover and create a romantic tone.

Reading and Communication Skills

Understand basic reading comprehension skills and key issues in writing and speaking

- Identify summaries or paraphrases of the main idea and supporting ideas in a selection

  - ▶ Recognize the primary argument
  - ▶ Restate the main point
  - ▶ Restate supporting points

- Identify how language is used and the meanings of words as they are used in context

  - ▶ Interpret contextual clues
  - ▶ Define an unfamiliar word based on its relation to similar words

- Identify how a selection is organized

  - ▶ Comparison and contrast
  - ▶ Main idea and evidence
  - ▶ Chronological sequence
  - ▶ Cause and effect
  - ▶ Problem and solution

- Distinguish fact from opinion

  - ▶ Recognize objective statements
  - ▶ Recognize subjective statements

- Make inferences and draw conclusions

  - ▶ Recognize possible outcomes or conclusions from evidence provided
  - ▶ Evaluate valid inferences or conclusions

- Understand the purposes for writing and speaking and the role of the audience within varying contexts

  - ▶ Recognize possible purposes, including
    - ◆ To appeal
    - ◆ To convince
    - ◆ To illustrate
    - ◆ To entertain
    - ◆ To explain
  - ▶ Understand roles of the audience, including
    - ◆ To listen/understand
    - ◆ To refute
    - ◆ To act

- Make decisions about the writing process, including identifying appropriate revision strategies for a given text

  - ▶ Identify steps in revision
  - ▶ Understand the use of transition words
  - ▶ Recognize where clarifying or expanding explanation is necessary

Exercise Related to the "Reading and Communication Skills" Topic

The following exercise and annotated sample are intended to give you practice in the kind of interpretive thinking about literature that is expected in the sections of the test described on the previous page. Although the format of this annotation exercise is not like that of the multiple-choice questions on the test, the skills of interpretation and evaluation needed to complete it are comparable. For this exercise, read the passage and questions and try to annotate the passage in the same way you annotated the E. B. White poem. Then, read the annotated version on the following page and compare your analysis.

★ *Here is a paragraph from an essay about the novels of Jane Austen. Read it and consider these questions: How does the writer establish the subject? How does he use specific examples to advance his argument? How does he communicate his own opinion about Austen's choice of subject matter?*

Austen's novels are relentlessly concerned with private life, concerned with "three or four families in a country town," as she put it in one famous letter. This is all the more remarkable when we consider the events of her lifetime. Though living through a period that witnessed the birth of an independent United States, the French Revolution, the Napoleonic Wars, and the upheavals of the Industrial Revolution, she focuses on a few middling gentry families in rural England. Touches of the wider world sometimes impinge on Austen's peaceful outposts—Wickham, a soldier, plays a prominent role in *Pride and Prejudice*; there are passing references to the British colonies and the slave trade in *Mansfield Park*; and the British navy's preservation of England in the Napoleonic Wars is duly noted in *Persuasion*. For the most part, though, her characters go about their farming and their business, their follies and especially their romances, their dances and their games of backgammon and whist, as if nothing has changed. Soldiers and sailors, when they appear, are always on leave.

★ *Here is the same paragraph with annotations that relate to the questions asked on the previous page.*

Austen's novels are relentlessly concerned with private life, concerned with "three or four families in a country town," as she put it in one famous letter. This is all the more remarkable when we consider the events of her lifetime. Though living through a period that witnessed the birth of an independent United States, the French Revolution, the Napoleonic Wars, and the upheavals of the Industrial Revolution, she focuses on a few middling gentry families in rural England. Touches of the wider world sometimes impinge on Austen's peaceful outposts—Wickham, a soldier, plays a prominent role in *Pride and Prejudice*; there are passing references to the British colonies and the slave trade in *Mansfield Park*; and the British navy's preservation of England in the Napoleonic Wars is duly noted in *Persuasion*. For the most part, though, her characters go about their farming and their business, their follies and especially their romances, their dances and their games of backgammon and whist, as if nothing has changed. Soldiers and sailors, when they appear, are always on leave.

The words "relentlessly" and "remarkable" communicate the author's surprise that Austen's works do not deal with historical events.

The phrases "wider world" and "peaceful outposts" make a strong contrast.

The opening sentence establishes the major theme of the passage, gaining support from Austen's own words.

Numerous examples illustrate the political, economic, and spiritual turmoil of Austen's era.

These are examples of the few times Austen does incorporate references to larger world events into her novels.

These examples lend weight to the argument that Austen was mainly concerned with domestic matters.

Study Topics: Mathematics

The mathematics section of the *Fundamental Subjects: Content Knowledge* test focuses on key indicators of general knowledge and understanding. It requires you to utilize fundamental skills that are founded upon broad concepts, as outlined in the list of topics below, which are based on The National Council of Teachers of Mathematics' document *Principles and Standards for School Mathematics*.

The test questions do not require knowledge of advanced-level mathematics vocabulary. You may use a nonprogrammable calculator while taking the test; a basic four-function calculator will be adequate.

Here is an overview of the areas covered in the "Mathematics" section:

Number Sense and Basic Algebra
- Compute using rational numbers
- Use estimating skills to solve a problem
- Use percents to solve a problem
- Set up ratios and simplify to solve a problem
- Set up and solve proportions
- Solve a word problem
- Express a word problem in algebraic form
- Represent and use numbers in equivalent forms
- Apply place-value concepts and numeration to ordering and regrouping

Geometry and Measurement
- Convert, select, and use measurements within the same system
- Use scale measurements to interpret maps, drawings, and models
- Use concepts of area, perimeter, circumference, and volume to solve a problem
- Solve a problem involving rates

Data Analysis and Probability
- Interpret data based on charts, graphs, tables, and spreadsheets
- Find trends and patterns and make inferences using graphs and data
- Determine the mean, median, mode, and range of sets of data
- Compare, calculate, and use probability in a variety of problems

Context

Since the focus of the mathematics section of the *Fundamental Subjects* test is on assessing the mathematical competencies needed in teaching and everyday life, each question is presented in one of the following three meaningful real-world contexts—work (classroom setting), personal, or interdisciplinary.

Work (Classroom Setting):

Be able to apply mathematical skills identified in the content specifications to a variety of problems in a school/classroom setting, such as budgeting for a field trip, club, or school event, interpreting a class survey, or calculating grades.

Personal:

Be able to apply mathematical skills identified in the content specifications to a variety of problems in a personal setting, such as balancing a checkbook, determining the amount or cost of floor covering for a room, calculating the cost of purchases with taxes and/or shipping costs, and determining appropriate gratuities.

Interdisciplinary:

Be able to apply mathematical skills identified in the content specifications to a variety of problems in an interdisciplinary setting, such as interpreting census and/or meteorological data, recipes, and computer-related tasks such as resizing.

Number Sense and Basic Algebra

Compute using rational numbers

- Be able to perform computations involving the arithmetic operations of addition, subtraction, multiplication, and division applied to rational numbers such as

  ▶ Integers

★ Suppose that the temperature at a location increased from −4° F to 12° F. To find the net change in temperature, would you use the computation 12 − 4 = 8 ? Why or why not?

  ▶ Fractions

★ How can you tell by inspection whether a fraction (e.g., $\frac{203}{198}$) has a value greater than 1 ?

  Whether a fraction such as $\frac{39}{75}$ has a value greater than $\frac{1}{2}$?

  ▶ Decimals

★ Can the product of two positive numbers be less than either number? How can you divide a decimal by 1,000 without using a calculator or actually doing the division?

- Be able to solve real-world problems using rational numbers

★ If $\frac{10}{24}$ of an amount is budgeted for rent and $\frac{15}{36}$ of the same amount is budgeted for food, is the amount budgeted for rent different from the amount budgeted for food? How can you decide?

Use estimating skills to solve a problem

- Approximate numbers

★ To estimate the value of $\frac{4}{11}$ of $3,000, what is a convenient approximation for $\frac{4}{11}$?

- Round whole numbers and decimals

★ Round 27,653.2175 to various decimal places. If you are rounding an amount of money to the nearest tenth of a cent, which decimal place determines whether you should round up or down?

- Recognize when and how to round numbers in order to find an estimate or the closest approximation to the value of a quantity

★ If the population of a town increases from 99,843 to 124,982, what would be an appropriate approximation to use for the two population figures to obtain an estimate of the increase?

★ If you round the prices of each of 17 drugstore items to the nearest dollar, by how much could the total of your estimates differ from the total of the actual prices? By $8 ? By $9 ?

- Determine when it is appropriate to round numbers before performing a computation

★ If a person walks at a rate of 21 steps in 10 seconds, how can you decide by estimation that the person would complete more than 100 steps in 52 seconds?

- Apply estimation skills to check the reasonableness of your solution to a problem

★ To check the placement of the decimal point in the product 2.3 × 6.98, what would be an integer estimate of the value of the product?

Use percents to solve a problem

- Be familiar with the concept of percent and understand that percents are relative quantities

★ What does *percent* mean? What is the difference between 20 and 20% ?

★ If the price of a chair was reduced by 20% and the price of a table was reduced by 15%, was the price of the chair reduced by the greater amount?

- Express a percent in equivalent forms (e.g., as a fraction or a decimal)

★ What are equivalent ways to represent 48% ? What percents have a value less than 1 ? Greater than 1 ?

- Solve problems posed in a real-world setting and involving percents

★ Suppose 24% of the scores in an athletic competition are less than 5.8. What percent would represent all of the scores? How would you find the percent of scores greater than or equal to 5.8 ? Do you need to know the total number of scores? Why or why not?

- Find a percent of a number (25% of 60)

- Find a number when a percent is given (60 is 25% of what number?)

- Find what percent one number is of another number (What percent of 12 is 9 ?)

★ Is asking, "What percent of 12 is 9 ?" the same as asking, "What percent of 9 is 12 ?"

- Compute the percent increase or the percent decrease of a quantity

★ What is meant by "20% decrease"? If a quantity decreases by 20% and then increases by 20%, is the net change 0%? Why or why not?

★ Is an increase in weight from 160 pounds to 200 pounds a 20% increase or a 25% increase?

★ A newspaper reported that enrollment at School A decreased by 150% and enrollment at School B increased by 200%. Which part of this report could be accurate? Which part inaccurate? Explain.

Set up ratios and simplify to solve a problem

- Be familiar with the concept of ratio and ways to express ratio

★ Can a ratio have a value greater than 1 ? Is the ratio 3 to 7 the same as the ratio 7 to 3 ?

★ The ratio of 4 boys to 5 girls can be expressed by the fraction $\frac{4}{5}$. What are some other ways of expressing this ratio?

- Solve problems by setting up a ratio and simplifying the result

★ What feature of a ratio allows you to find the simplest equivalent form?

★ On a school committee, the ratio of the number of men to the number of women is 8 to 12. What is the ratio expressed in lowest terms? Could there be a total of 10 committee members? 36 ? In each case, why or why not?

Set up and solve proportions

- Be familiar with the concept of proportion

★ How is the concept of proportion related to the concept of ratio? How do the two concepts differ? How many terms does a proportion have?

★ Why is $\frac{2}{3} = \frac{9}{12}$ not a valid proportion? How could you change one of the numbers so that the proportion is true?

- Solve a proportion by the method of cross multiplying

★ In the proportion $\frac{4}{5} = \frac{n}{12}$ what is the value of $5n$?

- Solve problems by setting up and solving a proportion

★ What does it mean to say that an amount of an ingredient in a recipe is *proportional* to the number of servings? Can you think of other situations in which one quantity is proportional to another quantity?

★ What does it mean for one quantity to be *inversely proportional* to another quantity? Can you think of quantities that are inversely proportional?

Solve a word problem

Note that since all questions in the Mathematics section are posed in a real-world setting, as described above under "Context," you should be able to

- Decide from a given verbal setting what types of calculation to perform in order to solve the problem posed

★ What arithmetic operation is indicated by the term "cumulative amount"? By "withdrawal"?

★ Prepare a list of mathematical terms and everyday words related to each of the arithmetic operations.

★ If Ms. Jones budgets $\frac{1}{4}$ of her monthly income for rent and $\frac{1}{3}$ of the remaining amount for food, what calculation would you need to perform to find the fraction of her monthly income that Ms. Jones budgets for food? Why is the answer *not* $\frac{1}{3}$?

Most questions are multi-step problems, that is, problems involving more than one computation. Therefore, you should be able to

- Determine not only what calculations to perform, but also the order in which to perform them

★ Suppose Bob has more than $10, spends $8.25, and then gives half of the remaining amount to Tom. Would Bob have the same amount remaining if he had first given half of his money to Tom and then spent $8.25 ?

- Recognize the various strategies for solving mathematical problems (e.g., drawing a picture, working backwards, finding a pattern, or considering a special case or a similar simpler problem)

★ Write a problem that you could solve by "working backwards." Be sure to give the end result from which you work.

★ How could you use a similar simpler problem together with pattern recognition to find the units digit in the number 2^{400} without actually evaluating this number?

Express a word problem in algebraic form

- Be familiar with the language of basic algebra

★ Is $2n - 5$ the same as $2(n - 5)$? How could you check?

★ What is the difference between an expression and an equation?

- Translate a word problem into an algebraic expression

★ There are n students in Ms. Smith's class. In Mr. Chen's class, there are 5 fewer than twice as many students as in Ms. Smith's class. Write an expression in terms of n for the number of students in Mr. Chen's class.

★ Suppose that 2 buses, each with a seating capacity of k people, transport a total of n people. One bus is full and the other bus has 2 empty seats. Do you see that $n = 2k - 2$ represents this situation? Can the situation also be represented by $2(k - 2)$?

- Solve a word problem by setting up a simple algebraic equation and solving the equation

★ In the bus problem above, if there are a total of 78 people on the two buses, how can you use the equation $n = 2k - 2$ to find the seating capacity of each bus? Could there be a total of 67 people on the two buses instead of 78 ?

Represent and use numbers in equivalent forms

- Recognize and represent numbers in equivalent forms

★ Are $\frac{1}{2}$, 0.5, and $\frac{30}{60}$ equivalent?

- Find a fraction that is equivalent to a given decimal

★ In a fractional equivalent of 12.037, if the numerator is 12,037, what is the denominator?

■ Find a decimal that is equivalent to a given fraction

★ How could you use the fact that the fraction $\frac{125}{40}$ represents an arithmetic operation to find a decimal equivalent?

★ Can every fraction be expressed as a fraction having some power of 10, such as 100 or 1,000 or 10,000, for its denominator? What are some fractions that you could use to decide?

■ Solve problems, such as comparing the relative sizes of quantities, by expressing numerical quantities in equivalent forms

---

★ Of 20 test grades, $\frac{1}{4}$ are A's, 9 are B's, 20% are C's, and the remaining grades are D's. What would be a convenient common form in which to express these quantities in order to decide which grade occurred most frequently?

■ Check answers by approximating solutions without actually doing all the work

---

★ How can you tell by inspection that the decimal equivalent of $\frac{14}{27}$ is approximately 0.5 ? If you are changing $\frac{44}{31}$ to a decimal, why must its value be greater than 1 ?

Apply place-value concepts and numeration to ordering and grouping

■ Solve problems using place-value concepts and numeration

★ In the decimal system of numeration, what is the ratio of the value of each digit to the value of the digit immediately to its right?

★ In the number 82.537, the place value of the digit 8 is how many times the place value of the digit 7 ?

■ Apply the concepts of place value and numeration to determine the order of magnitude of numbers (e.g., recognize that 1 million is 0.001 times 1 billion, or that $0.003 = \frac{3}{1000}$)

★ How can you use place value to determine which is greater, a water rate of \$0.012 per gallon or a water rate of \$0.0085 per gallon?

★ If you were asked to order the three meter readings 0.2340781, 0.234165, and 0.23419, which digits in each of the readings would it suffice to check to make a determination?

■ Apply the process of regrouping in solving problems that involve denominate numbers (measurements)

★ To find the time, in hours, that has elapsed from 11:45 A.M. to 6:25 P.M. on the same day, could either of the following computations be used to find the answer? Why or why not?

$$\begin{array}{r} 11.45 \\ -\ 6.25 \\ \hline \end{array} \qquad \begin{array}{r} 18\frac{5}{12} \\ -11\frac{3}{4} \\ \hline \end{array}$$

Geometry and Measurement

Convert, select, and use measurements within the same system

- Convert from one unit of measure to another (within the same system)

    ▶ Using nonmetric (U.S. customary) units of measure

    ★ What number should you use to change a measurement in feet to an equivalent measurement in yards? What arithmetic operation would be involved? If y feet $= z$ yards, is y less than, equal to, or greater than z?

    ▶ Using metric units

    ★ How are metric units related to each other (e.g., a millimeter and a centimeter)?

- Select and use appropriate units of measurement to solve real-world problems

    ★ What are some situations in which you might have to convert from one unit of measure to a different unit? What is an appropriate nonmetric unit of measure for the dimensions of a book? What is an appropriate metric unit of measure for the dimensions of a large city?

    ★ Beth is paid every 2 weeks and John is paid every month. If the amount of John's paycheck is twice the amount of Beth's, can it be determined which of the two has the greater annual salary? What relationship between different units of measure can help you decide?

Use scale measurements to interpret maps, drawings, and models

- Apply scale measurements to interpret maps, drawings, and models

    ▶ Scaling measurements involving length

    ★ What does it mean to say that the floor plan of a house is drawn to a scale in which 0.1 inch represents 1 foot? How could you use some of the ideas from the previous topic ("Convert, select, and use measurements within the same system") to determine how the dimensions of the house compare with the dimensions from the floor plan?

    ▶ Scaling measurements involving area

    ★ On a map of a city, if 5 centimeters represents 2 kilometers, how would you determine the scaling factor to use to find the area of a park in the city?

    ▶ Scaling measurements involving volume

    ★ In a scale model of a rectangular building, if each linear dimension of the model scales up by a factor of 10, by what factor does the volume of the building scale up? By what factor does the surface area of the building scale up?

    ★ If you wanted to make a scale model of a mountain, which would be a more appropriate geometric solid to use, a cylinder or a cone? Why? How could you determine the distance around the base of the mountain as predicted by your model?

Use concepts of area, perimeter, circumference, and volume to solve a problem

- ■ Solve problems by applying geometric concepts of measurement such as

  - ▶ The perimeter of a triangle or rectangle

  ★ How does the perimeter of the shaded region below compare with the perimeter of the entire rectangle? Do you need to know any measurements to decide?

  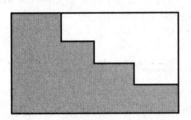

  - ▶ The area of a triangle or rectangle

  ★ Why is the sum of the areas of the shaded triangles in the figure below equal to $\frac{1}{2}$ the area of the entire rectangle?

  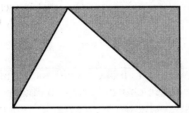

  - ▶ The circumference of a circle

  ★ Does the ratio of the circumference of a circle to its radius depend on the size of the circle? Why or why not?

  - ▶ The area of a circle

  ★ Suppose you wanted to find the area of the shaded region below (i.e., the region between the two circles). What measurement would you need to know? If you knew the circumference of each of the two circles, could you find the area? How about vice versa?

  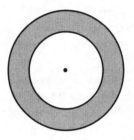

  - ▶ The volume of a solid such as a cylinder or rectangular solid

  ★ If a water tank has the shape of a cylinder as shown below left, what measurements would you need to know in order to compute the volume? What if the tank has the shape of a rectangular solid as shown below right? Could you find the volume if you knew only the total surface area (i.e., the sum of the areas of all six rectangular faces)?

  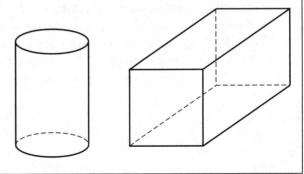

Solve a problem involving rates

- Express rates in equivalent forms (Also see the topic "Represent and use numbers in equivalent forms" above.)

★ What are some different ways to express rates? How is a rate related to a ratio?

- Solve problems by applying the concept of graduated rate

  ▶ Understand that a graduated rate scale is a series of different rates whose application depends on an increasing amount (e.g., sales commission)

★ What are some other situations in which you might have to apply a graduated rate scale?

★ If a parking garage charges $3.50 for the first hour and $1.50 for each hour thereafter, up to a maximum charge of $14.00, how does the total charge for 10 hours of parking compare with the total charge for 8 hours of parking?

- Solve problems by applying other kinds of rates

  ▶ Understand an important and common type of rate, the rate associated with a quantity that varies over time (e.g., the production rate of a machine or the speed of an object)

★ How are distance traveled, rate (speed), and time traveled related? How would the rate be expressed in terms of the distance and time?

★ The rate at which an object travels is called the *average speed*; however, you CANNOT compute average speed by taking the average (arithmetic mean) of individual rates. If a car travels at 30 miles per hour for half of the distance traveled and at 50 miles per hour for the other half, then the average speed for the entire distance is *not* 40 miles per hour, or the average (arithmetic mean) of the two rates. Why not? Why is the average speed actually less than 40 miles per hour?

The remarks above show that, since rates (including percents) are relative quantities, care must be exercised when computing with rates.

- Compare rates

★ Assess the claim that an interest rate of 6% is 2% "more than" an interest rate of 4%. How would you compare an interest rate of 6% with an interest rate of 4% ?

Data Analysis and Probability

Interpret data based on charts, graphs, tables, and spreadsheets

- Select the appropriate data to solve a problem

- Read and interpret data in any of several different formats

  - Charts or graphs, including
    - Pictographs
    - Line graphs

★ The data from what types of situations can be displayed effectively using a line graph?

  - Bar graphs

★ In a bar graph, what feature of each of the bars is pertinent to the data represented? Is the area of each bar relevant?

  - Circle graphs

★ If you used a circle graph to depict the results of a survey of ice-cream preferences, how would you indicate that 7 of the 28 students in the survey liked strawberry ice cream best?

★ Which type of graph is most useful for showing the distribution of a family's monthly expenses?

  - Tables

★ What are some advantages in presenting data in a table as opposed to using one of the types of graphs discussed above? What are some disadvantages?

- Frequency table

★ Consider the list of values 1, 2, 0, 4, 1, 3, 3, 1, 2, 0, 4, 5, 2, 3, 2, 3, 2, 4, 1, 2, 3, 0, 2, 3, 1. These values could represent the number of children in each of 25 families. Group these data into a two-column table with the first column listing each different value (x) and the second column listing the frequency (f) of occurrence for each of these different values. Do you see how the table you constructed provides a quick summary of the data? It also simplifies the calculation of certain statistical measures such as average, median, mode, etc. (See the topic "Determine the mean, median, mode, and range of sets of data" below.)

  - Know that for some sets of measurements it is convenient and informative to display the measurements in this special kind of table
  - Spreadsheets
    - Understand that a spreadsheet displays data in rows and columns, where the values in two or more columns are related by formulas

★ What are some examples of sets of data that can be analyzed using spreadsheets?

★ A storeowner creates a spreadsheet to analyze the store's inventory of purchases. If one column is headed "Item," a second column headed "Number Purchased," and a third column headed "Price per Unit Purchased," what formula relates the entries in the second and third columns? If these values are used for a fourth column, what would be an appropriate heading for the column?

Find trends and patterns and make inferences using graphs and data

- Discern patterns

★ If 2, 4, 6, 8, and 10 are the first five numbers in a list, must the sixth number be 12 ? Would your answer change if you were told that the numbers are generated by a formula? Suppose the list above represented a child's accumulated savings, in dollars, at the end of each successive week. What would you need to know to be able to find the savings at the end of the 10th week?

- Solve problems by finding trends

★ A certain quantity in an experiment doubles every 15 seconds. How could you use this pattern of behavior to determine how many times as much of the quantity there will be after 2 minutes?

- Solve problems by finding patterns

★ Suppose the water level of a river rose at a constant rate during a 24-hour period. If you knew the water level at the end of the 6th hour and also at the end of the 12th hour, could you determine the water level after the 20th hour? If so, how?

- Draw inferences based on trends and patterns contained in visual displays of data such as those discussed in the topic "Interpret data based on charts, graphs, tables, and spreadsheets" above

★ If the amount of a quantity changes with time and is represented in a graph as a straight line, what can you infer about the change in the quantity during two different 1-hour time periods?

Determine the mean, median, mode, and range of sets of data

- Apply the concept of average (arithmetic mean)

★ Is the average of three different numbers ever greater than any one of them? Why or why not?

★ Is it possible to find the average of 8 numbers without knowing the numbers themselves?

- Apply the concept of weighted average

★ How is a weighted average similar to the simple average, or arithmetic mean, mentioned above? When would it be appropriate to find a weighted average?

★ Suppose 7 of 12 scores are closer to 100 than to 60. Can you conclude that the average of the 12 scores is greater than 80 ?

- Find the median of a set of data

★ Can you compute the median of 20 home prices if you know the sum of the prices, but not the prices themselves?

★ How can you find the median of a set of data that is displayed in a frequency table (see under the topic "Interpret data based on charts, graphs, tables, and spreadsheets" above)? If there are 7 different values and they are given in increasing order, must the median be equal to the 4th value?

- Use the concept of mode

★ Can a set of data have more than one mode? More than one median? Can you think of one or more situations in real life in which knowing the mode of a set of data would be useful?

- Determine the range of a set of data

★ What numbers in a set of data does the range of data depend on? Can the range be less than the least number in the set? More than the greatest number?

★ Is it possible for the range of a set of data to be 0 ? What if there are at least two different numbers in the set?

- Solve problems that relate two or more of the statistical measures above

★ Can the median be equal to the average? If one value in a set is much larger (or smaller) than the others, which would be affected, the average or the median?

★ Which would be a more appropriate statistic to use in reporting annual family income in the United States in a given year—the average or the median?

Compare, calculate, and use probability in a variety of problems

- Calculate simple probability

★ Can the probability of an occurrence be equal to 2 ? Equal to 1 ? In each case, why or why not? What does it mean to say that the probability is 0 that a student to be selected at random from a group will be a boy? That the probability is $\frac{1}{2}$?

★ Suppose you want to find the probability that a ball to be selected at random from a box of solid-colored balls will be green. What different kinds of information would be sufficient? Would it be sufficient to know the total number of balls in the box? To know the fraction of balls in the box that are red?

- Solve problems by applying properties of the concept of probability

★ Continuing with the situation above of the balls in the box, how could you find the probability that the ball to be selected will be green if you were told the fraction of balls in the box that are *not* green?

Study Topics: Citizenship and Social Science

The "Citizenship and Social Science" section of the *Fundamental Subjects: Content Knowledge* test focuses on understanding important social, economic, cultural, and political concepts, geographical thinking, the workings of governmental systems, important historical events, and contributions of notable individuals within their historical and cultural contexts. The areas within this field are mutually enriching and interdependent, and questions on the test will often require knowledge and integration of two or more areas.

The "Citizenship and Social Science" section of the test specifically covers the following areas: historical continuity and change; people, places, and geographic regions; civics and government; and scarcity and economic choice.

Here is an overview of the areas covered in the "Citizenship and Social Science" section:

Historical Continuity and Change

- Chronological thinking skills
- Analysis of historical data
- Fact and opinion in historical documents
- Multiple points of view in historical documents
- Historical artifacts, oral traditions, and historical places
- Impact of individuals, groups, religions, social organizations, and movements on history
- Causes, results, and consequences of social, political, military, and economic events

People, Places, and Geographic Regions

- Use of maps, graphs, and charts to demonstrate geographic literacy
- Interaction between people and places
- Impact of human activity on the physical environment
- The environment's impact on people's lives and culture
- Human adaptation to the environment

Civics and Government

- How major systems of government function
- Major features of the United States political system
- Rights and responsibilities of United States citizens

Scarcity and Economic Choice

- Economic factors and principles that affect individuals, institutions, nations, and events
- How economic factors interact with geographic features, cultural values, and other factors

Historical Continuity and Change

This area of the test will evaluate your ability to demonstrate knowledge of historical events in United States and world history and to employ a number of skills related to the understanding of these events.

Be prepared to recognize these events, people, movements, and trends; make connections and comparisons among them; and interpret graphic material and written selections relating to them.

Chronological thinking skills

- Explain the impact and consequences resulting from important events that occurred on the following dates in world history:

    ▶ 220 and 476 C.E.
    ▶ 1492
    ▶ 1750–1780
    ▶ 1789
    ▶ 1914–18
    ▶ 1939–1945
    ▶ 1989

    (If you cannot find these on your own, see the list on p. 53.)

- Explain the impact and consequences resulting from important events that occurred on the following dates in United States history:

    ▶ 1607
    ▶ 1776
    ▶ 1787
    ▶ 1803
    ▶ 1861–1865
    ▶ 1917–1918
    ▶ 1929
    ▶ 1941–1945

- Consider the importance of understanding the chronology of events to comprehend cause and effect relationships and interactions between contemporaneous events

★ Compare the two lists of dates in United States and world history above. Which dates are identical or overlap? What is the significance of these identical or overlapping dates?

★ Make your own timeline of major events in United States and world history. Your world-history timeline will start with events that occurred in the period referred to as Before the Common Era (B.C.E.). The outline of United States history will begin with the 1400's. Keep in mind that Native Americans were here for thousands of years before that. Put each of the events listed below on your timeline in the correct century, and then describe important trends in political, military, social, religious, and economic history.

Analysis of historical data

- Interpret maps, graphs, and tables in United States and world history textbooks that illustrate political or military events, and economic development or demographic trends for events in the approximate time periods below

    ▶ United States maps
        ♦ Colonial trade
        ♦ Colonial boundaries
        ♦ The United States in 1783
        ♦ Missouri Compromise (1820)
        ♦ Native American migrations (1820–1840)
        ♦ Territories acquired by the United States (1857–1899)
        ♦ United States population trends in the nineteenth and twentieth centuries

- ► World maps
  - ♦ Indus Valley civilizations
  - ♦ Mesoamerican civilizations
  - ♦ Major world trade routes
  - ♦ The spread of Buddhism
  - ♦ The Han dynasty
  - ♦ European exploration and colonization
  - ♦ Atlantic slave trade
  - ♦ Imperialism in Africa in the late nineteenth and the twentieth centuries
  - ♦ NATO and the Warsaw Pact during the Cold War
- ► United States history graphs and tables
  - ♦ Cotton production
  - ♦ Slave population
  - ♦ Division of resources between North and South before the Civil War
  - ♦ Output and price of wheat in the nineteenth century
  - ♦ Unemployment during the Great Depression
  - ♦ Family income and levels of education
- ► World history graphs and tables

Fact and opinion in primary and other historical documents

- ■ Distinguish between fact and opinion in speeches, essays, and debates involving such historical issues as
  - ► The adoption of the United States Constitution
  - ► Emancipation Proclamation
  - ► Gettysburg Address
  - ► *Plessy* v. *Ferguson* decision
  - ► *Brown* v. *Board of Education* decision

> ★ Why did opponents of the United States Constitution insist on the addition of the Bill of Rights to the Constitution before agreeing to support it?

Multiple points of view in historical documents

- ■ Analyze multiple points of view found in primary and other historical documents, including essays, speeches, and personal narratives such as
  - ► Lincoln-Douglas debates over popular sovereignty
  - ► The conflicting arguments on whether to join the League of Nations
  - ► The contrasting points of view on what economic policy to follow to end the Great Depression
  - ► The national debate on the policy of isolationism prior to the attack on Pearl Harbor in the Second World War
  - ► The conflicting legal opinions in *Plessy* v. *Ferguson* and *Brown* v. *Board of Education*
- ■ Explain the importance of historical artifacts, oral traditions, and historical places, such as religious holy sites and ancient cities
  - ► Mecca
  - ► Medina
  - ► Jerusalem
  - ► Babylon
  - ► Chichen Itzá
  - ► Tenochtitlán
  - ► Machu Picchu
  - ► Rosetta stone
  - ► Hieroglyphics
  - ► Dead Sea scrolls

- ▶ Code of Hammurabi
- ▶ Pyramids and Valley of the Kings
- ▶ Great Wall of China
- ▶ Upanishads
- ▶ Qur'an (Koran)

★ Identify each of the documents, locations, or artifacts above and explain its significance, as well as the group or religion for which it had significance. What can be learned about different cultures or religions from each item?

Impact of individuals, groups, religions, social organizations, and movements on history

Causes, results, and consequences of social, political, military, and economic events

This section includes both movements and events from early civilizations until the present. Questions from this section may be based on events that happened prior to the voyages of Christopher Columbus, movements and events throughout the history of the United States, or world movements and events in which the United States was an integral participant.

- ■ Be familiar with major characteristics and achievements of early civilizations, including
  - ▶ Mesopotamia
  - ▶ Indus River Valley
  - ▶ China
  - ▶ Japan
  - ▶ Sub-Saharan Africa
  - ▶ Central and South America
  - ▶ Ancient Egypt
  - ▶ Greece
  - ▶ Rome

★ What are the principal economic, technological, social, and cultural advancements or practices for which each of the civilizations above is well known?

- ■ Be familiar with movements in the development of modern Europe
  - ▶ Renaissance
  - ▶ Reformation
  - ▶ Scientific revolution
  - ▶ Enlightenment

★ Explain how the lives and works of the following individuals helped to shape the modern world: Leonardo daVinci, Michelangelo, Sir Isaac Newton, Copernicus, Galileo, Martin Luther, John Locke.

- ■ Be familiar with events in the development of modern Europe and colonial America
  - ▶ Voyages of exploration
    - ◆ Marco Polo
    - ◆ Magellan
    - ◆ Christopher Columbus
    - ◆ Vasco da Gama
  - ▶ Causes, purposes, and results of exploration and colonization of North America by Spain, France, and England
  - ▶ Interaction between Native Americans and Europeans

★ What were the goals and objectives of early explorers in their voyages? What discoveries and knowledge did they draw on to aid them in their explorations?

- Be familiar with movements in the American Revolutionary War period
  - Causes of the American Revolution
  - Major ideas in the Declaration of Independence
  - The Articles of Confederation
  - Key individuals, including their major roles and beliefs
    - King George III
    - John Adams
    - George Washington
    - Benjamin Franklin
    - Thomas Jefferson
    - Thomas Paine
  - The adoption of the Constitution, including the key issues resolved by compromises and the addition of the Bill of Rights

★ What were the strengths and weaknesses of the Articles of Confederation?

★ What legislation passed under the Articles of Confederation permanently affected the territorial composition of the United States?

- Be familiar with events in the American Revolutionary War period
  - French and Indian War
  - Stamp Act, Tea Act, Intolerable Acts
  - Boycotts, Boston Massacre, Boston Tea Party
  - Major military events of the Revolutionary War

- Be familiar with international movements in the late eighteenth and the nineteenth centuries
  - Latin American independence movements
  - French Revolution and its impact
  - Industrial Revolution
    - Steam engine
    - Factory system
  - Imperialism
  - Meiji Restoration in Japan

★ Why did the Industrial Revolution create a desire among European powers for overseas colonies in Africa, Asia, and the Pacific Rim?

- Be familiar with movements involving the United States in the late eighteenth and nineteenth centuries
  - Industrial Revolution
    - Cotton gin
    - Steam locomotive
    - Fulton's steamboat
  - Abolitionist movement
    - Harriet Beecher Stowe
    - Harriet Tubman
    - Frederick Douglass
    - William Lloyd Garrison
  - Women's rights movement
    - Seneca Falls Convention
    - Susan B. Anthony
    - Dorothea Dix
    - Lucretia Mott
    - Elizabeth Cady Stanton
    - Sojourner Truth

★ In addition to women's rights, which nineteenth-century reform movements heavily involved women?

- ► Jacksonian Democracy
- ► United States policy toward Native Americans and responses of Native Americans
- ► Immigration and the Nativist movement
- ► Populist movement

★ Which groups banded together to form the Populist movement after the American Civil War? How successful were they in achieving their goals?

- ■ Be familiar with events involving the United States in the late eighteenth and the nineteenth centuries
  - ► War of 1812
  - ► Monroe Doctrine
  - ► Westward expansion, Indian removal and manifest destiny

★ Explain how each of the geographical areas encompassing the 50 states of the United States came under the jurisdiction of the United States government.

- ► Civil War-era events
  - ♦ Congressional attempts to balance slave and free states prior to the Civil War
  - ♦ Major events leading to the secession of the southern states and the war

♦ Key figures during the Civil War period and their impact, including
- • Abraham Lincoln
- • John Brown
- • Stephen Douglas
- • Ulysses Grant
- • Jefferson Davis
- • Robert E. Lee

★ What effects did the following have on the compromises attempted by Congress to keep the nation together prior to the American Civil War?

- ► The Dred Scott decision (1857) in the United States Supreme Court
- ► Discussion of "popular sovereignty" in the Lincoln-Douglas debates (1858)

- ► Reconstruction
  - ♦ Disputed election of 1876
  - ♦ Jim Crow laws
- ► Urbanization and technological progress
- ► Formation of the large trusts
- ► Rise of the labor movement

- ■ Be familiar with twentieth-century movements and events outside the United States
  - ► Causes and consequences of the First World War
  - ► Revolutions
    - ♦ Russian
    - ♦ Mexican
    - ♦ Chinese

★ Describe the role of the following revolutionary leaders: Mao Zedong, Lenin, Stalin.

▶ Worldwide economic depression in the 1930's and the political, social, and economic impact

▶ Rise of communism in the Soviet Union and fascism in Germany, Italy, and Japan

★ What factors contributed to the emergence of communism in the Soviet Union and fascism in Germany, Italy, and Japan?

▶ Causes and consequences of the Second World War; the Holocaust

▶ Origin and meaning of the Cold War

▶ Post-Second World War decolonization in Africa and Asia

★ Identify the contributions made in modern independence movements by the following individuals: Nelson Mandela, Mohandas Gandhi.

▶ Increasing national autonomy in Europe behind the former Iron Curtain and the former Yugoslavia

♦ Eastern Europe

♦ Balkans

♦ Former Soviet republics

▶ Rise of a global culture and global economy

▶ Major scientific advances

♦ Atomic power

♦ Space travel

♦ Satellite technology

♦ Computers

♦ Internet

■ Be familiar with twentieth-century movements and events involving the United States

▶ America's imperialism at the turn of the century

▶ Spanish-American War

▶ Building of the Panama Canal

▶ Theodore Roosevelt's "Big Stick diplomacy"

▶ Progressive movement

♦ Progressive Era amendments (16th, 17th, 18th, and 19th)

♦ Women's suffrage movement

♦ Muckrakers

★ Why did the Progressives as a movement succeed in areas in which the Populists had failed?

▶ America's involvement in the First World War and postwar isolationism

▶ Migration of African Americans from the South during and after the First World War including short- and long-term outcomes

▶ Immigration legislation and the Nativist movement

▶ The Great Depression and the New Deal

♦ Causes of the Depression

♦ New Deal legislation and policies, including Social Security

★ Why were critics of the New Deal unhappy with the policies pursued by Franklin D. Roosevelt to end the Great Depression?

▶ America's role in the Second World War and consequences at home and abroad

♦ Key military events

♦ Internment of Japanese Americans

♦ Decision to drop the atomic bombs on Hiroshima and Nagasaki and the consequences

♦ Postwar economic conditions

★ How did the end of the Second World War affect population distribution, the birth rate, and the standard of living of the majority of Americans?

► Impact of the expansion of the Soviet Union and the emergence of a communist government in China after the Second World War
  ♦ Korean War
  ♦ Military alliances (NATO, Warsaw Pact)
  ♦ McCarthyism
  ♦ Vietnam War

★ How were the "domino theory" and the policy of containment used to justify military alliances and the involvement of the United States in the world during the Cold War?

► Social and political movements
  ♦ Civil Rights movement
    — *Brown* v. *Board of Education*
    — Montgomery bus boycott
    — Martin Luther King Jr.
  ♦ Women's movement
  ♦ Environmental movement
  ♦ Peace movement
► Social policy initiatives
  ♦ "Great Society"
  ♦ "War on Poverty"
  ♦ Medicare

Significance of dates listed on p. 47.

■ 220 and 476 C.E.	Fall of Han dynasty and fall of western Roman Empire
■ 1492	Columbus lands in the Americas
■ 1750–1780	Height of the Atlantic slave trade
■ 1789	The French Revolution
■ 1914–1918	The First World War
■ 1939–1945	The Second World War
■ 1989	Fall of the Berlin Wall

People, Places, and Geographic Regions

This area of the test will evaluate your ability to use basic geographic skills to interpret maps, charts, and globes and to identify and evaluate the relationships between human and physical systems, the ways in which people adapt to the environment, and the impact of the environment on people.

Be prepared to demonstrate knowledge of basic geographic landforms and types of bodies of water and major examples of each type.

Be prepared to demonstrate knowledge of the effects of the interaction between human systems and physical systems.

Basic geographic literacy skills

- Read and interpret different kinds of maps and images

  - ▶ Physical maps
  - ▶ Topographical maps
  - ▶ Political and weather maps
  - ▶ Aerial photographs
  - ▶ Satellite images

- Use geographic tools such as atlases, databases, charts, graphs, and maps to interpret information

- Be familiar with latitude and longitude and their purposes

- Locate the equator and the international date line

- Use map legends to estimate distances, calculate scale, identify patterns represented in maps, and compute population density

- Describe and distinguish between the kinds of geographic features that make up Earth (continents, oceans, seas, rivers, bays, mountain ranges, plateaus, valleys, plains, ice caps, tundra, forest, grassland, desert, islands)

- Locate on a map all seven continents, the four oceans, major seas and rivers, and major mountain ranges

---

★ How do the coordinates of latitude and longitude help to establish the location of a place on Earth?

★ Explain how Earth's parallels and meridians are organized.

Interaction between people and places

- Be familiar with natural resources—what they are and why they matter

  - ▶ Renewable and nonrenewable resources
  - ▶ Energy, mineral, food, and land resources

- Be familiar with ecosystems and why understanding ecosystems is important

- Apply geography to an understanding of the historical development of people and their cultures

---

★ Distinguish between renewable and nonrenewable resources.

★ Classify each of the following as a renewable or nonrenewable resource: minerals, forests, fossil fuels, animal life.

★ How can geography be helpful in interpreting past or present events or situations such as the westward movement in the United States, Cold War strategy, and contemporary conflicts in the Middle East?

★ How can geography help us to understand the consequences of artificially-created political boundaries?

Impact of human activity on the physical environment

- Understand the effects of human-initiated changes on the environment
  - ▶ Water and air pollution
  - ▶ Waste disposal
  - ▶ Logging, deforestation, erosion, and desertification
  - ▶ Global warming and ozone-layer depletion

★ What are the causes and consequences of deforestation and desertification?

★ What techniques or practices can be used to prevent or reduce the negative impacts of deforestation and desertification?

The environment's impact on people's lives and culture

- Know the basic mechanisms and consequences of physical changes that have short-term effects on Earth, including floods, droughts, and snowstorms

- Know the basic mechanisms and consequences of physical changes that have long-term effects on Earth, including earthquakes (plate tectonics) and natural erosion

- Understand the impact of the environment on human systems such as
  - ▶ Essentials like food, clothing, and shelter
  - ▶ Transportation and recreation
  - ▶ Economic and industrial systems

★ Explain how the following climates differ from one another: tropical, dry, middle latitude, high latitude, and highland.

Human adaptation to the environment

- Understand factors affecting settlement patterns—why some places are densely populated and others sparsely populated

- Be familiar with major population trends in the United States in the nineteenth and twentieth centuries

Civics and Government

This area of the test will evaluate your knowledge of different forms of government, the functions of government, methods of implementing governmental decision making at different levels, and rights and responsibilities of citizens in the United States.

How major systems of government function

- Know the definition of "government"

- Understand reasons why government is needed (conflict resolution, collective decision making, etc.)

- Know how governments are created and changed

- Be familiar with political theory and theorists such as Montesquieu, Hobbes, Locke, Marx, and Lenin

- Be familiar with international organizations such as the United Nations

- Understand forms of government
  - ▶ Unitary structures
  - ▶ Confederacy
  - ▶ Federalism
  - ▶ Parliamentary systems

★ How do modern political thinkers who favor constitutional democracies differ from their predecessors on the origins of the power to govern and how power should be distributed?

★ Compare and contrast the views of twentieth-century political theorists and revolutionaries on the origins of the power to govern and how power should be distributed.

★ How does the operation of parliamentary systems of government differ from presidential forms of government?

★ In what way did the concepts expressed in the Magna Carta and the Mayflower Compact contribute to the development of the rights of individuals as they are legislated in the United States today?

Major features of the United States political system

Questions will be asked involving excerpts from the Declaration of Independence and the Constitution. Questions will also be asked about major ideas in these documents or about the specific roles and responsibilities of the federal government.

- Be familiar with the Articles of the United States Constitution and the amendments to the Constitution, including the Bill of Rights

- Define the "separation of powers" among the three branches of the federal government and the major responsibilities of each branch

- Understand various procedures in the United States Constitution

  ▶ Passage of legislation

  ▶ Confirmation of federal judges and cabinet officials

  ▶ Amending the Constitution

  ▶ Impeachment and removal of officials from office

  ▶ Composition and functioning of the Electoral College

- Be familiar with landmark Supreme Court decisions

- Be able to define major responsibilities of state and local governments

★ How do the procedures established in the Constitution to ratify a treaty or to declare war illustrate the principle of checks and balances?

★ How does the distribution of powers in the Constitution—in what political scientists refer to as expressed, implied, concurrent, and reserved powers—affect the relationship between the federal government and the states?

★ Which United States Supreme Court cases have been considered landmark cases in the areas of civil rights, the right to privacy, and the rights of accused persons? What important legal principles did they establish?

★ What are some examples of laws dealing with rights and privileges commonly exercised by individuals that vary from state to state?

Rights and responsibilities of United States citizens

- Understand the meaning and importance of the following rights of democratic citizens

  - Freedom of speech
  - Freedom of religion
  - Freedom of press
  - Freedom of assembly
  - Freedom to petition
  - Right to privacy

- Recognize the importance of the following economic rights

  - Property rights
  - The right to choose one's work
  - The right to join or not join a labor union
  - The right to apply for copyrights and patents

- Understand the formation of political parties and the process for selecting and electing candidates

- Understand the need to balance citizens' rights with the common good

- Be familiar with citizens' legal obligations (to obey the law, serve as a juror, and pay taxes) and civic-minded obligations (becoming informed about issues and candidates, voting, volunteering, and serving in the military or alternative service)

- Understand the naturalization process by which immigrants become citizens of the United States

---

★ What does the expression "majority rule with minority rights" mean? How is it applied to government decision making in the United States?

Scarcity and Economic Choice

This area of the test will evaluate your ability to demonstrate knowledge of fundamental economic concepts and to employ economic principles to answer questions about economic decision making, including the interpretation of graphic and tabular economic data.

Economic factors and principles that affect individuals, institutions, nations, and events

- Identify basic economic concepts and apply economic principles to economic situations

  - Types and functions of economic systems
    - Command
    - Market
    - Mixed economies
  - Scarcity
  - Needs and wants
  - Supply and demand
  - Price determination for goods and services in a market economy
  - Factors of production (land, labor, and capital)
  - Business cycle (expansion and contraction)
  - Inflation and deflation
  - Employment, unemployment, and the "labor force"
  - Attempts to modify free market decisions
    - Price floors
    - Price ceilings
    - Cost-of-living adjustments (COLA's)

- Interpret graphs, maps, and charts providing information about employment/unemployment rates, currency exchange rates, rates of inflation or deflation, and distribution of wealth

- Understand division of labor and specialization

- Distinguish between private and public goods and services

- Recognize incentives in a capitalist economy

    ▶ Private ownership
    ▶ Private enterprise
    ▶ The profit motive

- Be familiar with the effects of rapid technological change and international competition on labor in general and on individuals

- Be familiar with international economics

    ▶ Imports and exports
    ▶ Tariffs, subsidies, and quotas
    ▶ Economic sanctions
    ▶ Arguments for and against "free trade"
    ▶ Currencies and exchange rates: the effects when the United States dollar gains or loses value relative to other currencies

---

★ How does the implementation of measures such as the minimum wage and rent controls demonstrate attempts to modify the operation of the laws of supply and demand?

★ What are some key ways in which division of labor and specialization improve people's lives?

★ How does an increase or decrease in the international value of the dollar affect the demand for American-made products outside the United States?

Study Topics: Science

The "Science" section of the *Fundamental Subjects: Content Knowledge* test focuses on general background knowledge and understanding of the fundamental facts, basic concepts, principles, processes, methods, and skills that are common to the various scientific disciplines.

Because conceptual and procedural schemes unify scientific disciplines, the following concepts and processes can be found within any of the other specific content domains:

- Systems, orders, and organization

- Evidence, models, and explanation

- Change, constancy, and measurement

- Evolution and equilibrium

- Form and function

The "Science" section of the test specifically covers the following topic areas: nature and history of science; basic principles and fundamentals of science; and science, technology, and social perspectives.

Here is an overview of the areas covered in the "Science" section:

Nature and History of Science ——————

Gathering reliable information about nature and developing explanations that can account for the information gathered

Identifying and using the elements of scientific inquiry for problem solving

The heritage of science

Processes involved in scientific data collection, manipulation, interpretation, and presentation

Interpreting and drawing conclusions from data

Analyzing errors in data that are presented

Basic Principles and Fundamentals of Science —

> Using basic principles of science to explain natural phenomena and events
>
> Energy relationships and transformations in both living and nonliving contexts
>
> Structure and properties of matter and the forces that act upon it
>
> Diversity and characteristics of living organisms and their interactions with the environment and each other
>
> Processes that have led to changes in the dominant organisms at various times and in various places
>
> Earth as a part of the universe and as a body with specific features and processes

Science, Technology, and Social Perspectives —

> Impact of science and technology on the environment and human affairs
>
> Societal issues with health awareness and medical advances
>
> Social, political, ethical, and economic issues arising from science and technology
>
> Relationships between societal demands and scientific and technological enterprises

Nature and History of Science

Science involves the investigation of nature and the processes that are observed in the natural world; therefore, skills dealing with inquiry and investigation are an integral part of studying and understanding science. The skills necessary to perform scientific investigations include the ability to collect and analyze data, form conclusions based on data and observations, and propose solutions to problems that arise in scientific studies. Scientific investigations and discoveries of historical significance are also included within this topic.

Gathering reliable information about nature and developing explanations that can account for the information gathered

A variety of sources may be used to investigate what is already known about a topic, but these sources should be evaluated for their reliability and validity. After a basic understanding is obtained through research, experiments and field studies may be conducted and analyzed to more fully comprehend the natural world.

- Use print and electronic sources of information

- Evaluate reliability and validity of information, e.g., comprehensiveness of evidence and logic

- Perform experiments and field studies

- Synthesize information from all sources to develop explanations for observations

★ What methods could be used to obtain accurate quantitative data about the deer population in a local community over a three-year period?

★ Assuming that the deer population increased by 25 percent over three years, list other pieces of information, and their respective sources, that might be helpful in explaining the observed change.

Identifying and using the elements of scientific inquiry for problem solving

Scientific inquiry refers to the ways in which scientists investigate questions that have been posed or observations that have been made. It involves a systematic method of approaching the question or problem being addressed, but is not a rigid sequence of steps.

- Propose questions for investigations and/or make observations

- Form hypotheses

- Design experiments or evaluate the design of an experiment, e.g., evaluate the use of control variables and experimental variables

- Evaluate experimental results and draw conclusions to accept or reject the hypothesis

★ How are control variables and experimental variables used in scientific investigations?

★ Design an experiment to examine the effect of temperature on seed germination.

The heritage of science, that is, important scientific events and contributions made by major historical figures

Important historical events in science provide a framework for understanding current scientific investigations and perspectives on societal and technological changes over time, e.g., Charles Darwin's theory of natural selection and Isaac Newton's explanation of gravity.

★ How has most scientific work been built on earlier knowledge over the centuries?

★ Why was acceptance of some major scientific explanations so difficult (e.g., those of Copernicus, Galileo, Darwin)?

Processes involved in scientific data collection, manipulation, interpretation, and presentation

It is important to use appropriate instruments or tools to collect data and to use proper procedures for making accurate and precise measurements. Once these observations and data have been collected, mathematical operations may be performed with the data, and then both observations and data need to be interpreted to discover relationships among the variables being investigated or to determine the significance of the observations that have been made. Scientists often communicate the results of their investigations by using charts, tables, or graphs to summarize their observations and data.

- Construct appropriate graphs of data, e.g., a line graph for continuous data, a bar graph for categorical or discontinuous data

- Data interpretation, e.g., direct versus inverse relationships between variables

★ What are some examples of measuring instruments?

★ Which graphic method of presentation would be most suitable for illustrating the relative amounts of solid waste that are recycled, incinerated, and disposed of in landfills?

Interpreting and drawing conclusions from data, including those presented in tables, graphs, maps, and charts

The ability to understand and interpret data is an important skill in many fields and plays a role in decision making in both school and life situations. Additionally, the logic and merit of conclusions presented on the basis of data should be evaluated.

- Identify patterns or trends in data

- Make predictions from data, e.g., extrapolate or interpolate from the trend line on a graph, use the equation for the line when data appears to be linear

- Form conclusions based on data

★ The following graph presents data for atmospheric carbon dioxide concentrations and change in average global temperature for over 160,000 years. Based on the graph, what conclusion can be reached?

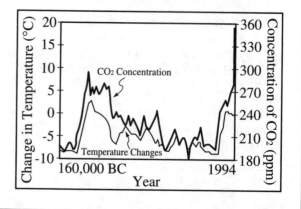

★ The following table provides information regarding the crops planted on farmland, the management of the land, and earthworm populations in a certain state. Use this data to describe the relationship between plowing the land and the number of earthworms per acre of land.

Crop	Management	Earthworm per Acre
Continuous corn	Plow	40,000
	No-till	75,000
Continuous soybean	Plow	230,000
	No-till	500,000

Analyzing errors in data that are presented

Experimental data have potential for containing errors from various sources. Data should be evaluated for possible sources of errors.

- Review the experimental procedure for likely sources of procedural error

- Compare data for various trials, e.g., evaluate reproducibility of measurements

- Determine the magnitude of errors when accepted value is known, e.g., absolute error is the difference between accepted value and experimental value; percent error is absolute error as a percent of the accepted value

★ The experimental values obtained for the boiling point of three samples of distilled water were 93°C, 91°C, and 88°C. What are possible sources of errors in the experiment above if the accepted value for the boiling point of water is 100°C?

Basic Principles and Fundamentals of Science

Scientific literacy can be established by applying basic principles of science and demonstrating the understanding of fundamental facts and concepts in the various scientific disciplines. The basic principles of science are unifying concepts and processes common to all content areas. While these principles are important as a common theme, specific fundamental content knowledge of the major disciplines is also necessary to demonstrate scientific literacy.

Using basic principles of science to explain natural phenomena and events

Scientific fields differ in their content, but there are common principles that may be used to understand and explain the phenomena that are observed in all content areas. A working knowledge of these principles improves understanding in all content areas and increases the ability to explain phenomena and events.

★ Why do we see our breath on a cold day but not on a warm day?

★ Why does rubbing your hands together make them warmer?

Energy relationships and transformations in both living and nonliving contexts

Energy exists in many forms and is necessary for life processes and nonliving systems. An understanding of the relationships among the forms of energy and the storage, transformations, and passage of energy through living and nonliving systems is critical to understanding of the processes that involve energy.

- Be familiar with forms of energy, e.g., potential energy, kinetic energy, chemical energy, mechanical energy

- Be familiar with transfer and conservation of energy

- Be familiar with energy in living systems, e.g., photosynthesis, cellular respiration, energy flow in an ecosystem

- Be familiar with energy in nonliving systems, e.g., phase changes, production of ocean currents and weather systems by solar energy

---

★ How is the energy of a rock sitting on the top of a hill different from the energy of a rock sitting at the bottom of the same hill?

★ How does the energy associated with a bicycle change as it speeds up going downhill?

Structure and properties of matter and the forces that act upon it

The properties of matter and the changes that it undergoes can easily be observed at the macroscopic level, but to comprehend why matter has particular properties and goes through physical and chemical changes, it is necessary to understand its structure at the atomic level.

- Be familiar with the physical properties of matter, e.g., phases of matter

- Be familiar with the chemical properties of matter, e.g., atoms, elements, molecules, compounds, mixtures, and solutions

- Be familiar with the conservation of matter

- Be familiar with the physical and chemical changes of matter

---

★ Does air take up space?

★ Sometimes when two chemicals are combined, a chemical reaction takes place. What are some of the signs of such a chemical reaction?

- Be familiar with forces acting on matter
  - ▶ Types of forces, e.g., electrostatic attraction between oppositely charged particles, gravitational forces, and magnetic forces
  - ▶ Types of motion, e.g., linear motion, circular motion
  - ▶ Newton's laws of motion
  - ▶ Friction
  - ▶ Equilibrium

★ A balloon is rubbed on a sweater and placed near a narrow stream of running water. Explain why the stream of water is deflected toward the balloon.

★ Compare the frictional force experienced when a box of textbooks is pushed across a floor and a bicycle is pushed across the same floor.

★ Understand the basic difference between photosynthesis and cellular respiration.

★ List three organelles within the cell and identify the function of each.

★ Compare the relative number of chromosomes in a cell that has undergone mitosis with one from the same organism that has undergone meiosis.

Diversity and characteristics of living organisms and their interactions with the environment and each other

Living organisms possess several common characteristics, yet the differences among the organisms are significant enough to allow classification into major and minor groups based on their differences. Survival of individual organisms as well as the species requires organisms to interact with each other and with their environment.

■ Be familiar with the characteristics of living organisms

▶ Structure and function, e.g., basic function of a cell, groups of cells forming tissues and organs in multicellular organisms

▶ Energy use and metabolism, e.g., chemical reactions required for life, energy required for organization

▶ Maintenance of a constant internal environment, e.g., constant body temperature, maintenance of blood pH within a narrow range

▶ Reproduction, growth, and development, e.g., reproduction strategies among organisms, genetic material from one versus two parents

▶ Response to environmental stimuli

■ Recognize that the classification system of organisms is based on anatomical and biochemical similarities, as well as evolutionary history

▶ Classification hierarchy—kingdom, phylum, class, order, family, genus, and species

▶ Binomial nomenclature for naming organisms

★ What is the fundamental difference, at the cellular level, between a corn plant and a bacterium?

★ The scientific name for a dog is *Canis familiaris*. What level of classification is indicated by the name "*Canis*"?

■ Be familiar with interactions between organisms, e.g., competition for resources and space, understanding concepts of food web and food chain, specific types of interactions

■ Be familiar with interactions between organisms and their environment

★ What are the roles of producers and decomposers in a food web?

★ Wolves are predators that prey on deer. How has the deer population responded in areas where wolves have been eradicated?

Processes that have led to changes in the dominant organisms at various times and in various places

Species evolve over time as a result of genetic variation, competition for resources, and the differing survival and reproductive capacities of different organisms.

- Be familiar with evidence for evolution, e.g., fossil record, molecular or biochemical similarities

- Be familiar with natural selection versus artificial selection by selective breeding

★ Cytochrome c, a complex protein required for cellular respiration, is more similar in monkeys and cows than it is in monkeys and fish. What does this suggest about the relationship between monkeys and cows as compared to that between monkeys and fish?

Earth as a part of the universe and as a body with specific features and processes

Earth operates as a collection of interconnected systems that may be changing or may be relatively stable in the short term but that are in dynamic equilibrium over the long term. Cycles involving matter and energy are key to the maintenance of the planet and its climate. As a part of a solar system, galaxy, and universe, Earth is also affected by other planets and stars.

- Be familiar with the origin and evolution of the universe

- Be familiar with the components of the universe, e.g., galaxies, solar systems, stars

- Be familiar with Earth as a component of the solar system, e.g., the relationship between the Sun, Earth, and Earth's moon, Earth's rotation on an axis and revolution around the Sun, the seasons

- Be familiar with the processes that occur on Earth and shape the planet, e.g., geochemical cycles, matter that moves through atmosphere, oceans, solid Earth, organisms, plate tectonics

★ Why do the coldest temperatures in the Northern Hemisphere occur during the month of January even though Earth is closer to the Sun in January than it is in July?

★ How does nitrogen, the most abundant element in Earth's atmosphere, become incorporated into biological molecules in organisms?

Science, Technology, and Social Perspectives

Scientific knowledge and its subsequent technological applications have significantly influenced our environment and our lives in both positive and negative ways. These scientific advances may exact a cost, however, as they may create new problems even as they solve existing ones.

Impact of science and technology on the environment and human affairs (e.g., production, use, and management of energy, consumer products, and natural resources)

- Be familiar with energy production, use, and management, e.g., use of fossil fuel and nuclear power plants

■ Be familiar with consumer products, e.g., use of plastics, chloroflurocarbons (CFCs) from refrigerants and aerosol cans, antibiotics, and other pharmaceuticals

■ Be familiar with natural resources, e.g., water pollution by heavy metals or pesticides, air pollution such as acid precipitation (deposition), photochemical smog, and land use such as habitat destruction

★ What is the environmental impact of the increased level of carbon dioxide in the atmosphere as a result of the combustion of fossil fuels for energy?

★ Describe the connection between chloroflurocarbons (CFCs) and the increased risk of skin cancer.

Societal issues with health awareness and medical advances (including biotechnology)

Discoveries in the medical field and the introduction of new medical technologies, including biotechnology, have provided promise for previously untreatable medical conditions while unleashing tremendous debate with respect to the impact on society.

■ Be familiar with the discovery and use of antibiotics

■ Be familiar with the use of transplanted and artificial organs, e.g., economic cost to society, availability based on ability to afford treatment

■ Be familiar with reproductive technology, e.g., economic cost to society for procedures, ethical questions with respect to this technology

■ Be familiar with biotechnology

  ► Ethical considerations relating to applications of genetic engineering, e.g., cloning organisms and genetically modified organisms

  ► Tangible benefits to society, e.g., source of large quantities of insulin and some antibiotics, improved strains of crop plants

★ Compare the societal issues related to using genetic engineering to develop a tomato that will remain firm when it ripens and using a genetically engineered tomato to help correct defective genes in a human, allowing the individual to have a normal life.

Social, political, ethical, and economic issues arising from science and technology

The study of science and the development of technological endeavors do not occur in isolation from society but rather have an impact on society and are in turn influenced by societal issues. Piloted space exploration, for example, has affected many aspects of society, but the frequency and nature of this exploration have also been affected by political, ethical, and economic considerations.

■ Recognize political and ethical issues related to decision making in the design of technology

■ Be familiar with social and economic issues related to food preparation and safety

■ Be familiar with the effect of politics on the future of nuclear power plants and disposal of radioactive waste

★ Identify the social, political, and economic issues related to the mass production of fuel-cell powered automobiles.

Relationships between societal demands and scientific and technological enterprises (e.g., past and current trade-offs, social change as a result of scientific and technological advances)

There is an ongoing desire to solve problems throughout the world using scientific knowledge and its application in technological enterprises. The use of technology should involve an assessment of the risks, benefits, and costs as well as the impact on society of implementing new technology.

■ Understand that the implementation of technology consists of a decision-making process, e.g., weighing costs and benefits with respect to environment, economy, humans, health

★ Describe the costs and benefits of maintaining a habitable space station.

★ List the economic and environmental trade-offs of solar energy sources.

Chapter 5

Practice Questions for the *Fundamental Subjects: Content Knowledge* Test

▶ ▶ · ▶ ▶ ▶ ▶ ▶ ▶ ▶ ▶ ▶ ▶

Now that you have worked through strategies relating to multiple-choice questions and have studied the content topics, you should take the following practice test. You will probably find it helpful to simulate actual testing conditions, giving yourself 96 minutes to work on the questions. You can cut out and use the answer sheet provided if you wish.

Keep in mind that the test you take at an actual administration will have different questions, although the proportion of questions in each area and major subarea will be approximately the same. You should not expect the percentage of questions you answer correctly on this practice test to be exactly the same as when you take the test at an actual administration, since numerous factors affect a person's performance in any given testing situation.

When you have finished the practice questions, you can score your answers and read the explanations of the best answer choices in chapter 6.

THE **PRAXIS**
S E R I E S™

TEST NAME:

Fundamental Subjects: Content Knowledge

Practice Questions

Time—96 minutes
80 Questions

(Note: At the official test administration, there will be 100 questions,
and you will be allowed 120 minutes to complete the test.)

Answer Sheet C

(ETS)

THE PRAXIS SERIES

DO NOT USE INK

Use only a pencil with soft black lead (No. 2 or HB) to complete this answer sheet.
Be sure to fill in completely the oval that corresponds to the proper letter or number.
Completely erase any errors or stray marks.

1. NAME
Enter your last name and first initial.
Omit spaces, hyphens, apostrophes, etc.

Last Name (first 6 letters)   F I

(A through Z ovals grid)

2.

YOUR NAME:
(Print)

Last Name (Family or Surname)   First Name (Given)   M. I.

MAILING ADDRESS:
(Print)

P.O. Box or Street Address   Apt. # (if any)

City   State or Province

Country   Zip or Postal Code

TELEPHONE NUMBER: ( ) Home   ( ) Business

SIGNATURE: _____   **TEST DATE:** _____

3. DATE OF BIRTH

Month	Day
Jan.	
Feb.	
Mar.	
April	
May	
June	
July	
Aug.	
Sept.	
Oct.	
Nov.	
Dec.	

4. SOCIAL SECURITY NUMBER

(Ovals 0–9)

5. CANDIDATE ID NUMBER

(Ovals 0–9)

6. TEST CENTER / REPORTING LOCATION

Center Number   Room Number

Center Name

City   State or Province

Country

7. TEST CODE / FORM CODE

(Ovals 0–9)
0
1

8. TEST BOOK SERIAL NUMBER

9. TEST FORM

10. TEST NAME

MH04167   Q2573-06   51055 • 08920 • TF74E400

202974

1 2 3 4

CERTIFICATION STATEMENT: (Please write the following statement below. DO NOT PRINT.)
"I hereby agree to the conditions set forth in the *Registration Bulletin* and certify that I am the person whose name and address appear on this answer sheet."

_____

_____

_____

SIGNATURE: _____ DATE: _____ / _____ / _____
Month   Day   Year

BE SURE EACH MARK IS DARK AND COMPLETELY FILLS THE INTENDED SPACE AS ILLUSTRATED HERE: ● .

#	A	B	C	D		#	A	B	C	D		#	A	B	C	D		#	A	B	C	D
1	Ⓐ	Ⓑ	Ⓒ	Ⓓ		41	Ⓐ	Ⓑ	Ⓒ	Ⓓ		81	Ⓐ	Ⓑ	Ⓒ	Ⓓ		121	Ⓐ	Ⓑ	Ⓒ	Ⓓ
2	Ⓐ	Ⓑ	Ⓒ	Ⓓ		42	Ⓐ	Ⓑ	Ⓒ	Ⓓ		82	Ⓐ	Ⓑ	Ⓒ	Ⓓ		122	Ⓐ	Ⓑ	Ⓒ	Ⓓ
3	Ⓐ	Ⓑ	Ⓒ	Ⓓ		43	Ⓐ	Ⓑ	Ⓒ	Ⓓ		83	Ⓐ	Ⓑ	Ⓒ	Ⓓ		123	Ⓐ	Ⓑ	Ⓒ	Ⓓ
4	Ⓐ	Ⓑ	Ⓒ	Ⓓ		44	Ⓐ	Ⓑ	Ⓒ	Ⓓ		84	Ⓐ	Ⓑ	Ⓒ	Ⓓ		124	Ⓐ	Ⓑ	Ⓒ	Ⓓ
5	Ⓐ	Ⓑ	Ⓒ	Ⓓ		45	Ⓐ	Ⓑ	Ⓒ	Ⓓ		85	Ⓐ	Ⓑ	Ⓒ	Ⓓ		125	Ⓐ	Ⓑ	Ⓒ	Ⓓ
6	Ⓐ	Ⓑ	Ⓒ	Ⓓ		46	Ⓐ	Ⓑ	Ⓒ	Ⓓ		86	Ⓐ	Ⓑ	Ⓒ	Ⓓ		126	Ⓐ	Ⓑ	Ⓒ	Ⓓ
7	Ⓐ	Ⓑ	Ⓒ	Ⓓ		47	Ⓐ	Ⓑ	Ⓒ	Ⓓ		87	Ⓐ	Ⓑ	Ⓒ	Ⓓ		127	Ⓐ	Ⓑ	Ⓒ	Ⓓ
8	Ⓐ	Ⓑ	Ⓒ	Ⓓ		48	Ⓐ	Ⓑ	Ⓒ	Ⓓ		88	Ⓐ	Ⓑ	Ⓒ	Ⓓ		128	Ⓐ	Ⓑ	Ⓒ	Ⓓ
9	Ⓐ	Ⓑ	Ⓒ	Ⓓ		49	Ⓐ	Ⓑ	Ⓒ	Ⓓ		89	Ⓐ	Ⓑ	Ⓒ	Ⓓ		129	Ⓐ	Ⓑ	Ⓒ	Ⓓ
10	Ⓐ	Ⓑ	Ⓒ	Ⓓ		50	Ⓐ	Ⓑ	Ⓒ	Ⓓ		90	Ⓐ	Ⓑ	Ⓒ	Ⓓ		130	Ⓐ	Ⓑ	Ⓒ	Ⓓ
11	Ⓐ	Ⓑ	Ⓒ	Ⓓ		51	Ⓐ	Ⓑ	Ⓒ	Ⓓ		91	Ⓐ	Ⓑ	Ⓒ	Ⓓ		131	Ⓐ	Ⓑ	Ⓒ	Ⓓ
12	Ⓐ	Ⓑ	Ⓒ	Ⓓ		52	Ⓐ	Ⓑ	Ⓒ	Ⓓ		92	Ⓐ	Ⓑ	Ⓒ	Ⓓ		132	Ⓐ	Ⓑ	Ⓒ	Ⓓ
13	Ⓐ	Ⓑ	Ⓒ	Ⓓ		53	Ⓐ	Ⓑ	Ⓒ	Ⓓ		93	Ⓐ	Ⓑ	Ⓒ	Ⓓ		133	Ⓐ	Ⓑ	Ⓒ	Ⓓ
14	Ⓐ	Ⓑ	Ⓒ	Ⓓ		54	Ⓐ	Ⓑ	Ⓒ	Ⓓ		94	Ⓐ	Ⓑ	Ⓒ	Ⓓ		134	Ⓐ	Ⓑ	Ⓒ	Ⓓ
15	Ⓐ	Ⓑ	Ⓒ	Ⓓ		55	Ⓐ	Ⓑ	Ⓒ	Ⓓ		95	Ⓐ	Ⓑ	Ⓒ	Ⓓ		135	Ⓐ	Ⓑ	Ⓒ	Ⓓ
16	Ⓐ	Ⓑ	Ⓒ	Ⓓ		56	Ⓐ	Ⓑ	Ⓒ	Ⓓ		96	Ⓐ	Ⓑ	Ⓒ	Ⓓ		136	Ⓐ	Ⓑ	Ⓒ	Ⓓ
17	Ⓐ	Ⓑ	Ⓒ	Ⓓ		57	Ⓐ	Ⓑ	Ⓒ	Ⓓ		97	Ⓐ	Ⓑ	Ⓒ	Ⓓ		137	Ⓐ	Ⓑ	Ⓒ	Ⓓ
18	Ⓐ	Ⓑ	Ⓒ	Ⓓ		58	Ⓐ	Ⓑ	Ⓒ	Ⓓ		98	Ⓐ	Ⓑ	Ⓒ	Ⓓ		138	Ⓐ	Ⓑ	Ⓒ	Ⓓ
19	Ⓐ	Ⓑ	Ⓒ	Ⓓ		59	Ⓐ	Ⓑ	Ⓒ	Ⓓ		99	Ⓐ	Ⓑ	Ⓒ	Ⓓ		139	Ⓐ	Ⓑ	Ⓒ	Ⓓ
20	Ⓐ	Ⓑ	Ⓒ	Ⓓ		60	Ⓐ	Ⓑ	Ⓒ	Ⓓ		100	Ⓐ	Ⓑ	Ⓒ	Ⓓ		140	Ⓐ	Ⓑ	Ⓒ	Ⓓ
21	Ⓐ	Ⓑ	Ⓒ	Ⓓ		61	Ⓐ	Ⓑ	Ⓒ	Ⓓ		101	Ⓐ	Ⓑ	Ⓒ	Ⓓ		141	Ⓐ	Ⓑ	Ⓒ	Ⓓ
22	Ⓐ	Ⓑ	Ⓒ	Ⓓ		62	Ⓐ	Ⓑ	Ⓒ	Ⓓ		102	Ⓐ	Ⓑ	Ⓒ	Ⓓ		142	Ⓐ	Ⓑ	Ⓒ	Ⓓ
23	Ⓐ	Ⓑ	Ⓒ	Ⓓ		63	Ⓐ	Ⓑ	Ⓒ	Ⓓ		103	Ⓐ	Ⓑ	Ⓒ	Ⓓ		143	Ⓐ	Ⓑ	Ⓒ	Ⓓ
24	Ⓐ	Ⓑ	Ⓒ	Ⓓ		64	Ⓐ	Ⓑ	Ⓒ	Ⓓ		104	Ⓐ	Ⓑ	Ⓒ	Ⓓ		144	Ⓐ	Ⓑ	Ⓒ	Ⓓ
25	Ⓐ	Ⓑ	Ⓒ	Ⓓ		65	Ⓐ	Ⓑ	Ⓒ	Ⓓ		105	Ⓐ	Ⓑ	Ⓒ	Ⓓ		145	Ⓐ	Ⓑ	Ⓒ	Ⓓ
26	Ⓐ	Ⓑ	Ⓒ	Ⓓ		66	Ⓐ	Ⓑ	Ⓒ	Ⓓ		106	Ⓐ	Ⓑ	Ⓒ	Ⓓ		146	Ⓐ	Ⓑ	Ⓒ	Ⓓ
27	Ⓐ	Ⓑ	Ⓒ	Ⓓ		67	Ⓐ	Ⓑ	Ⓒ	Ⓓ		107	Ⓐ	Ⓑ	Ⓒ	Ⓓ		147	Ⓐ	Ⓑ	Ⓒ	Ⓓ
28	Ⓐ	Ⓑ	Ⓒ	Ⓓ		68	Ⓐ	Ⓑ	Ⓒ	Ⓓ		108	Ⓐ	Ⓑ	Ⓒ	Ⓓ		148	Ⓐ	Ⓑ	Ⓒ	Ⓓ
29	Ⓐ	Ⓑ	Ⓒ	Ⓓ		69	Ⓐ	Ⓑ	Ⓒ	Ⓓ		109	Ⓐ	Ⓑ	Ⓒ	Ⓓ		149	Ⓐ	Ⓑ	Ⓒ	Ⓓ
30	Ⓐ	Ⓑ	Ⓒ	Ⓓ		70	Ⓐ	Ⓑ	Ⓒ	Ⓓ		110	Ⓐ	Ⓑ	Ⓒ	Ⓓ		150	Ⓐ	Ⓑ	Ⓒ	Ⓓ
31	Ⓐ	Ⓑ	Ⓒ	Ⓓ		71	Ⓐ	Ⓑ	Ⓒ	Ⓓ		111	Ⓐ	Ⓑ	Ⓒ	Ⓓ		151	Ⓐ	Ⓑ	Ⓒ	Ⓓ
32	Ⓐ	Ⓑ	Ⓒ	Ⓓ		72	Ⓐ	Ⓑ	Ⓒ	Ⓓ		112	Ⓐ	Ⓑ	Ⓒ	Ⓓ		152	Ⓐ	Ⓑ	Ⓒ	Ⓓ
33	Ⓐ	Ⓑ	Ⓒ	Ⓓ		73	Ⓐ	Ⓑ	Ⓒ	Ⓓ		113	Ⓐ	Ⓑ	Ⓒ	Ⓓ		153	Ⓐ	Ⓑ	Ⓒ	Ⓓ
34	Ⓐ	Ⓑ	Ⓒ	Ⓓ		74	Ⓐ	Ⓑ	Ⓒ	Ⓓ		114	Ⓐ	Ⓑ	Ⓒ	Ⓓ		154	Ⓐ	Ⓑ	Ⓒ	Ⓓ
35	Ⓐ	Ⓑ	Ⓒ	Ⓓ		75	Ⓐ	Ⓑ	Ⓒ	Ⓓ		115	Ⓐ	Ⓑ	Ⓒ	Ⓓ		155	Ⓐ	Ⓑ	Ⓒ	Ⓓ
36	Ⓐ	Ⓑ	Ⓒ	Ⓓ		76	Ⓐ	Ⓑ	Ⓒ	Ⓓ		116	Ⓐ	Ⓑ	Ⓒ	Ⓓ		156	Ⓐ	Ⓑ	Ⓒ	Ⓓ
37	Ⓐ	Ⓑ	Ⓒ	Ⓓ		77	Ⓐ	Ⓑ	Ⓒ	Ⓓ		117	Ⓐ	Ⓑ	Ⓒ	Ⓓ		157	Ⓐ	Ⓑ	Ⓒ	Ⓓ
38	Ⓐ	Ⓑ	Ⓒ	Ⓓ		78	Ⓐ	Ⓑ	Ⓒ	Ⓓ		118	Ⓐ	Ⓑ	Ⓒ	Ⓓ		158	Ⓐ	Ⓑ	Ⓒ	Ⓓ
39	Ⓐ	Ⓑ	Ⓒ	Ⓓ		79	Ⓐ	Ⓑ	Ⓒ	Ⓓ		119	Ⓐ	Ⓑ	Ⓒ	Ⓓ		159	Ⓐ	Ⓑ	Ⓒ	Ⓓ
40	Ⓐ	Ⓑ	Ⓒ	Ⓓ		80	Ⓐ	Ⓑ	Ⓒ	Ⓓ		120	Ⓐ	Ⓑ	Ⓒ	Ⓓ		160	Ⓐ	Ⓑ	Ⓒ	Ⓓ

FOR ETS USE ONLY	R1	R2	R3	R4	R5	R6	R7	R8	TR	CS

FUNDAMENTAL SUBJECTS: CONTENT KNOWLEDGE

ENGLISH LANGUAGE ARTS

Directions: Each of the questions or incomplete statements below is followed by four suggested answers or completions. Select the one that is best in each case and fill in the corresponding lettered space on the answer sheet with a heavy, dark mark so that you cannot see the letter.

1. The following excerpt is from Garrison Keillor's *Leaving Home*.

> It snowed eight inches on Tuesday and if you'd been there and come for a walk with us you'd know why people in my town love stories so
> *Line* much. There was a fine dim light in the air: the
> 5 town was full of moonlight, the old streetlamps glowed, the houses were lit, light shone up from the snow, the snow on the trees—it was so absolutely wonderfully shining beautiful, it made you feel that anything could happen now.

The narrator supports the claim that "you'd know why people in my town love stories so much" (lines 2–4) by

(A) contrasting the warmth of indoors to the cold, snowy outdoors

(B) comparing the wintry appearance of the town to the setting of a familiar fairy tale

(C) describing how the beauty of the town leads to a sense of unlimited possibility

(D) providing examples of stories that townspeople tell in the cold of winter

Questions 2–3 are based on the following two poems.

The fog comes
on little cat feet.
It sits looking
over harbor and city
on silent haunches
and then moves on.

—Carl Sandburg, "Fog"

The yellow fog that rubs its back upon
  the windowpanes,
The yellow smoke that rubs its muzzle
  on the windowpanes
Licked its tongue into the corners of the evening,
Lingered upon the pools that stand in drains,
Let fall upon its back the soot that falls from
  chimneys,
Slipped by the terrace, made a sudden leap,
And seeing that it was a soft October night,
Curled once about the house, and fell asleep.

—T. S. Eliot, from "The Love Song of
J. Alfred Prufrock"

2. The poems are similar in that both
  (A) describe the fog as if it has animal characteristics
  (B) lament the darkness the fog brings to the land
  (C) focus on people's reactions to the fog
  (D) detail the strange way familiar objects look in the fog

3. In the second poem, it is suggested that the fog
  (A) has changed its color as the evening grows darker
  (B) has originated from the puddles on the street
  (C) will seep in through the windows of a house
  (D) will remain about the house for the night

4. The following excerpt is from Rudolfo Anaya's *Bless Me, Ultima.*

And I was happy with Ultima. We walked together in the llano and along the river banks to gather herbs and roots for her medicines. She taught me the names of plants and flowers, of trees and bushes, of birds and animals; but most important, I learned from her that there was a beauty in the time of day and in the time of night, and that there was peace in the river and in the hills.

In the excerpt, the author of the passage develops the character of Ultima by

(A) explaining where she gained her knowledge of plants and animals

(B) contrasting her tranquility with the speaker's restlessness

(C) discussing her ability to solve problems encountered by other characters

(D) describing what she taught the speaker about the natural world

Questions 5–6 are based on the following excerpt from a poem by Alfred Lord Tennyson.

Tears, idle tears, I know not what they mean,
Tears from the depth of some divine despair
Rise in the heart, and gather to the eyes,
In looking on the happy Autumn-fields,
And thinking of the days that are no more.

5. The speaker is expressing feelings of

(A) nostalgia
(B) frustration
(C) indecision
(D) contentment

6. The speaker uses the phrase "the depth of some divine despair" to indicate

(A) his sympathy for another's unhappiness

(B) his acknowledgment of his own wrongdoing

(C) the intensity of the feeling that inspires his tears

(D) the necessity for acceptance of divine retribution

7. The following excerpt is adapted from Alice Hoffman's *Turtle Moon*.

People in Verity like to talk, but the one thing they neglect to mention to outsiders is that something is wrong with the month of May. It isn't the humidity, or even the heat, which is so fierce and sudden it can make grown men cry. Every May, when the sea turtles begin their migration across West Main Street, mistaking the glow of streetlights for the Moon, people go a little bit crazy. Girls run away from home, babies cry all night, ficus hedges explode into flame, and during one particularly awful May, half a dozen rattlesnakes set themselves up in the phone booth outside the 7-Eleven and refused to budge until June.

The author uses details such as migrating sea turtles and ficus hedges bursting into flame to help portray Verity in May as

(A) isolated and lonely
(B) strange and distressing
(C) beautiful but dangerous
(D) overwhelmed by the fertility and new growth of spring

Questions 8–10 are based on the following excerpt from Gwendolyn Brooks's novel, *Maud Martha* **(1953).**

Up the street, mixed in the wind, blew the children, and turned the corner onto the brownish-red brick school court. It was wonderful. Bits of pink, of blue,

Line white, yellow, green, purple, brown, black, carried
5 by jerky little stems of brown or yellow or brown-black, blew by the unhandsome gray and decay of the double-apartment buildings, past the little plots of dirt and scanty grass that held up their narrow brave banners: PLEASE KEEP OFF THE GRASS—
10 NEWLY SEEDED. There were lives in the buildings. Past the tiny lives the children blew. Cramp, inhibition, choke—they did not trouble themselves about these. They spoke shrilly of ways to fix curls and pompadours, of "nasty" boys and "sharp" boys,
15 of Joe Louis, of ice cream, of bicycles, of baseball, of teachers, of examinations, of Duke Ellington, of Bette Davis. They spoke—or at least Maud Martha spoke—of the sweet potato pie that would be served at home.

8. The passage is primarily concerned with describing

   (A) children learning in a classroom
   (B) children's feelings about their families
   (C) children talking on the way to school
   (D) children playing a game

9. The children in the excerpt are characterized as

   (A) excited about a recent event in school
   (B) absorbed in their own interests
   (C) unfriendly toward each other
   (D) unwilling to attend school

10. The excerpt presents a contrast between the

   (A) bright colors of the children's clothes and the gray decay of the buildings
   (B) narrowness of the children's concerns and the larger world of celebrities
   (C) relaxed atmosphere of home and the stern discipline at school
   (D) pleasures of the children and the cares of their adult teachers

Questions 11–13 are based on the following excerpt from Ann Patchett's novel *Bel Canto*.

Many years later, when everything was business, when he worked harder than anyone in a country whose values are structured on hard work, he believed that life, true life, was something that was stored in music. True life was kept safe in the lines of Tchaikovsky's *Eugene Onegin* while you went out into the world and met the obligations required of you. Certainly he knew (though he did not completely understand) that opera wasn't for everyone, but for everyone he hoped there was something. The records he cherished, the rare opportunity to see a live performance, those were the marks by which he gauged his ability to love. Not his wife, his daughters, or his work. He never thought that he had somehow transferred what should have filled his daily life into opera.

Line marks 5, 10, 15 at left margin.

11. The excerpt is primarily concerned with

(A) describing a particular aspect of a character

(B) contrasting several characters' responses to music

(C) explaining how a character's passion for music led to an unusual event

(D) explaining how a character was influenced by an experience

12. In the phrase "somehow transferred what should have filled his daily life into opera" (lines 14–16), the narrator suggests which of the following about the character being described?

(A) He finds greater emotional satisfaction in music than in work or family.

(B) He assumes that his passion for music is shared by many other people.

(C) He devotes the majority of his time to his passion for music.

(D) He keeps the intensity of his passion for music secret from his wife and daughters.

13. The character is described in the passage as someone who

(A) loves to sing opera

(B) is an industrious worker

(C) has no talent for business

(D) encourages his family to enjoy opera

14. In my neighborhood graffiti seems to be born right out of the walls. It grows out of the gray concrete of highway overpasses like some strange decorative mold. It will appear within days on any fresh surface. Even in places where the artists could not possibly reach the wall, you would eventually spot huge, round, fat, silver-rimmed letters. Amazingly, despite the endless nights I spent sailing down those rivers of concrete, I never once saw anyone actually making the graffiti. How they did it I do not know.

The author's primary purpose in the passage is to

(A) argue that graffiti should be considered a legitimate art form

(B) reflect on the graffiti in his neighborhood and express wonder at its occurrence

(C) outline techniques graffiti artists use to create graffiti in high places

(D) denounce graffiti artists for their disrespect for public property

Questions 15–17 are based on the following passage from Jill Ker Conway's *The Road from Coorain*.

Line

At home, faced with the drudgery of cooking over a wood stove, laundering clothes in a copper heated by a wood fire, and baking bread after the day's work was over, [my mother's] mind turned sadly
5 to her starched white nurse's uniforms and the pleasures of being off duty. But she was no quitter. Her greatest strengths were an iron will and great powers of endurance. No standard of cleanliness or nicety of domestic arrangements was sacrificed
10 because of the limited supply of water, the outdoor privy, and the never-ending red dust. By six in the evening the children were bathed, the struggling geraniums watered, the dinner table set with starched linen and well-polished silver, and she was dressed
15 immaculately for dinner.

15. The author reveals her mother's character by

  (A) providing information about her mother's education

  (B) providing details about her mother's everyday life

  (C) describing her mother's background and upbringing

  (D) describing her mother's effect on the family's children

16. The sentence "But she was no quitter" (line 6) suggests that the author's attitude toward her mother is one of

  (A) indifference

  (B) admiration

  (C) resentment

  (D) perplexity

17. The author's mention of "the never-ending red dust" (line 11) serves primarily to

  (A) exemplify the obstacles her mother had to overcome

  (B) emphasize the dangers her mother faced every day

  (C) explain how her mother gained such great powers of endurance

  (D) reveal the futility of her mother's efforts

Questions 18–19 are based on the following excerpt from a book about playwriting.

If you want to be a serious writer, you will learn sooner or later to keep a writer's journal to record your thoughts and ideas. However, you will probably
Line use all other illogical systems first. You will probably
5 begin by trying the messy process of jotting hasty notes on any available napkin, envelope, or shopping list. Several months later these notes will surface and you will look at the notes in blank confusion while trying to recapture the flash of insight that prompted
10 your hurried scribbles.

18. The author uses the word "you" most likely to refer to a

 (A) student reviewing another student's work
 (B) teacher who wants to encourage students to keep a writer's journal
 (C) person who wants to be a serious writer
 (D) person who has published successfully

19. The author of the passage would most likely agree that the "process" mentioned in line 5 is

 (A) a good way to learn how to keep a writer's journal
 (B) a method practiced by writers who are highly organized
 (C) an outdated way of revising written work
 (D) an impractical way of recording thoughts and ideas

20. The idea seemed far-fetched at first. Expeditions to the North Pole are not new, of course. In recent years, they have been undertaken with increasing sophistication: snowmobiles instead of dogsleds, airplanes resupplying well-equipped teams. My plan was new: a solo journey to the world's magnetic North Pole, a journey on foot and no more equipment than I could pull on a sled. I would be the first woman to make such a journey.

Which of the following words, if inserted at the beginning of the fourth sentence ("My plan . . . a sled"), would best clarify its function in relationship to the rest of the paragraph?

 (A) Similarly,
 (B) For example,
 (C) In contrast,
 (D) Indeed

MATHEMATICS

21. Lin likes to keep an estimated total of what she has charged on her credit card. On a recent shopping trip, her charges were $212.56, $56.41, $5.17, and $10.74. Which of the following is the closest estimate of the total of these charges?

(A) $265
(B) $285
(C) $310
(D) $335

Questions 22–23 refer to the table below.

Erica's Class Schedule	
Period	Time
Homeroom	8:05 - 8:22
Period 1	8:26 - 9:48
Period 2	9:52 - 11:14
Lunch	11:18 - 11:48
Period 3	11:52 - 1:14
Period 4	1:18 - 2:40

22. According to Erica's class schedule, how many minutes long is period 2 ?

(A) 82
(B) 102
(C) 122
(D) 162

23. Erica's school day starts at the beginning of homeroom and ends at the end of period 4. How many <u>hours</u> long is her school day?

(A) $6\frac{7}{20}$

(B) $6\frac{7}{12}$

(C) $7\frac{1}{7}$

(D) $7\frac{5}{12}$

24. A cup of whole milk has 30 more calories than a cup of orange juice. If j represents the number of calories in a cup of orange juice, which of the following represents the number of calories in a cup of whole milk, in terms of j ?

    (A) $j + 30$

    (B) $j - 30$

    (C) $\dfrac{j}{30}$

    (D) $30j$

25. A plumber charges a flat fee of $36 per hour for work on weekdays and $48 per hour for work on Saturdays and Sundays. The plumber worked on a job for 4 hours last Friday, finished the job last Saturday, and charged a total of $288. How many hours did the plumber work last Saturday?

    (A) 3
    (B) 4
    (C) 6
    (D) 8

26. After Mr. Shaw graded the tests for his second-period class, he determined that the class average (arithmetic mean) was 75. A student who had been ill took the test at a later date and earned a grade that is 10 points higher than the class average. Which of the following statements must be true about the new class average?

    (A) It is lower than before.
    (B) It is less than 10 points higher than before.
    (C) It is 10 points higher than before.
    (D) Mr. Shaw cannot determine a new class average.

GIFT BASKET CONTENTS

Item	Number
Oranges	3
Apples	4
Plums	2
Walnuts	6
Candies	8

27. The table above shows the contents of each gift basket Mrs. Graham assembles. On a certain day, she has only 53 oranges. The greatest number of baskets that Mrs. Graham could assemble that day would require how many candies?

    (A) 124
    (B) 128
    (C) 136
    (D) 140

HADDOCK AND BASMATI RICE

2 lbs Haddock

2 cups Basmati Rice

$5\frac{1}{4}$ cups Fish Stock

2 Onions

Color	Number of Ping-Pong Balls
Red	125
Blue	75
Green	100
Yellow	150
White	50

28. Chris is making Haddock and Basmati Rice for his dinner guests. The partial list of ingredients shown above will yield 4 servings. If Chris wants to make 6 servings, how many cups of fish stock will he need?

(A) $6\frac{1}{4}$

(B) $6\frac{7}{8}$

(C) $7\frac{1}{4}$

(D) $7\frac{7}{8}$

29. At a fair a large container holds 500 Ping-Pong balls of various colors, as summarized in the table above. If one of the Ping-Pong balls is to be randomly selected from the container, what is the probability that the ball will be either blue or white?

(A) $\frac{1}{3}$

(B) $\frac{1}{4}$

(C) $\frac{1}{5}$

(D) $\frac{2}{5}$

30. A newspaper article reported that 62% of the 1,500 people who renewed their driver's licenses last month were 36 years old or older. How many were younger than 36 years old?

(A) 570
(B) 620
(C) 790
(D) 930

City	Annual Budget
A	$0.224 billion
B	$226.5 million
C	$218.9 million
D	$0.216 billion

31. The table above shows the annual budgets for four cities, with two budgets reported in millions of dollars and the other two budgets reported in billions of dollars. Which city has the smallest budget? (1 billion = 1,000,000,000)

   (A) A
   (B) B
   (C) C
   (D) D

32. On a map, $\frac{1}{2}$ inch corresponds to an actual distance of 5 miles. If a rectangular region on the map measures $1\frac{1}{2}$ inches by 4 inches, how many square miles of actual area does this region represent?

   (A) 450 square miles
   (B) 500 square miles
   (C) 550 square miles
   (D) 600 square miles

33. Bob's checking-account balance was $982. He then deposited a check for x dollars and took $35 out of the account. His new balance was $1,104. What was the value of x ?

   (A) 33
   (B) 87
   (C) 122
   (D) 157

34. The ratio of the number of male students to the number of female students in Cranston High School is 5 to 7. If there are 600 students in the school, how many are male students?

   (A) 180
   (B) 200
   (C) 250
   (D) 350

	Departed (local time)	Arrived (local time)
Flight 1	New York 2:32 P.M.	Chicago 2:55 P.M.
Flight 2	Chicago 3:40 P.M.	Los Angeles 5:46 P.M.

35. A trip from New York to Los Angeles required a stop in Chicago to change planes. The table above shows local times of arrival and departure for the two flights. If Chicago's local time is 1 hour earlier than New York's and 2 hours later than Los Angeles', what was the total time for the trip from New York to Los Angeles?

   (A) 6 hr 14 min
   (B) 6 hr 4 min
   (C) 5 hr 59 min
   (D) 5 hr 40 min

Behavior	Probability of Behavior
Peck the button	0.80
Peck things, but not the button	0.15
Do nothing	0.05

36. In an experiment, a pigeon can exhibit only one of the three behaviors shown in the table above. For each behavior, the table shows the probability that the pigeon will exhibit that behavior. If the experiment is repeated 40 times, what is the expected number of times that the pigeon's behavior will <u>not</u> be to peck the button?

(A)   2
(B)   4
(C)   6
(D)   8

Questions 37–38 refer to the graph below.

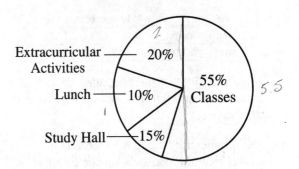

The circle graph above shows the percent distribution of the 10 hours that Gail spends at school during a typical day.

37. How many more hours does Gail spend in classes than in extracurricular activities?

(A) $2\frac{1}{2}$

(B)   3

(C) $3\frac{1}{2}$

(D)   4

38. What fraction of the time Gail spends at school is spent in study hall during a typical day?

(A) $\frac{1}{10}$

(B) $\frac{3}{20}$

(C) $\frac{1}{5}$

(D) $\frac{3}{10}$

Questions 39-40 refer to the table below.

Room	Dimensions (feet)
Living room	20 by 16
Family room	24 by 18

The dimensions of the McDades' rectangular living room and family room are shown in the table above.

39. The perimeter of the family room is how much greater than the perimeter of the living room?

   (A)   6 ft
   (B)   12 ft
   (C)   24 ft
   (D)   112 ft

40. If carpeting for the family room costs $20 per square yard, what is the total cost of the carpeting needed to cover the family room?

   (A) $920
   (B) $960
   (C) $1,050
   (D) $1,100

CITIZENSHIP AND SOCIAL SCIENCE

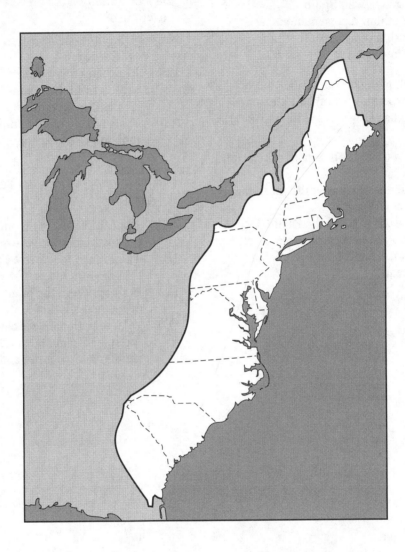

41. Which of the following dates best approximates the
time period represented by the political map above?

(A) 1607
(B) 1776
(C) 1812
(D) 1860

42. Which of the following was a major cause of the American Revolutionary War?

   (A) Border disputes with Spain
   (B) Taxation without representation
   (C) The expansion of slavery
   (D) Religious intolerance

43. Which of the following best describes the purpose of the expedition Thomas Jefferson selected Meriwether Lewis and William Clark to lead?

   (A) To survey a route for the transcontinental railroad
   (B) To navigate the Mississippi River to the city of New Orleans
   (C) To find a water route to the Pacific Ocean
   (D) To explore Panama as a possible source for a canal to connect the Atlantic and Pacific Oceans

44. Which of the following additions to the United States Constitution was adopted by amendment to place a limit on the powers of the federal government?

   (A) A limit to one four-year term on the presidency
   (B) Reserving to the states the power to secede from the Union
   (C) The Bill of Rights
   (D) A restriction on the number of terms an individual may serve in Congress

45. Which of the following was a significant factor contributing to the French Revolution in the late 1700's?

   (A) Opposition of the revolutionaries to the political ideas of the American Revolution
   (B) The French monarchy's policy of isolating France from the rest of Europe
   (C) A sharp fall in the price of bread, a staple of the peasant diet
   (D) A large national debt caused in part by foreign adventures and the need to support a large army and navy

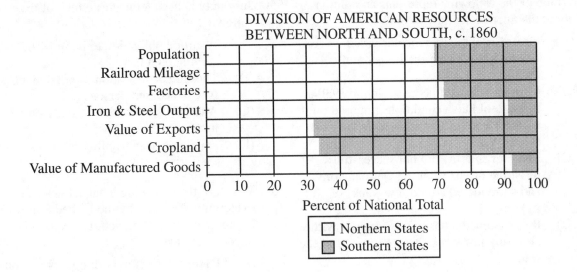

DIVISION OF AMERICAN RESOURCES
BETWEEN NORTH AND SOUTH, c. 1860

Percent of National Total

☐ Northern States
▨ Southern States

46. Which of the following statements about the Civil War era can be inferred from the graph above?

(A) The North had superior ability to produce war-making weaponry.

(B) The South had a larger population base for recruiting soldiers.

(C) The North and South had similar agricultural resources.

(D) The North had financial support from foreign trading partners.

47. Which of the following represents an opinion about the Second World War era?

(A) Great Britain and France declared war on Germany following the invasion of Poland.

(B) Germany turned to Nazism in the 1930's because of harsh conditions imposed on it by the Treaty of Versailles after the First World War.

(C) The French army did not successfully resist the offensive of the German army and surrendered after a few weeks of fighting.

(D) Russia signed a nonaggression pact with Germany just weeks before the start of the war.

- Indira Gandhi
- Golda Meir
- Margaret Thatcher

48. Which of the following best describes the individuals listed above?

(A) Social reformers
(B) Political leaders
(C) Scientists
(D) Educational theorists

49. Which of the following is a shared or concurrent power exercised by the federal and state governments in the United States?

(A) Raising an army and navy
(B) Levying taxes on income
(C) Issuing driver's licenses
(D) Imposing tariffs on imported goods

50. Jury duty is best defined as which of the following?

(A) A juror's obligation to be impartial when serving on a jury
(B) The state's obligation to provide a trial by jury to accused persons
(C) A citizen's obligation to serve on a local jury
(D) A judge's responsibility to choose jurors for a trial

51. Which of the following legal actions can overcome a decision by the United States Supreme Court that an act of Congress is unconstitutional?

(A) Passing the act in both houses of Congress by a three-fourths vote
(B) Amending the Constitution to permit the provision or provisions of the act declared unconstitutional
(C) Removing the Supreme Court justices who voted against the act, by a vote of censure
(D) Asking the President to suspend the power of the Supreme Court to conduct judicial review of the law

52. Which of the following is a power officially granted to the United Nations?

(A) Approving the constitutions of newly formed governments
(B) Regulating trade among nation-states
(C) Legitimizing international response against aggressor nations
(D) Controlling international migration

POPULATION DENSITY OF THE CONTIGUOUS UNITED STATES

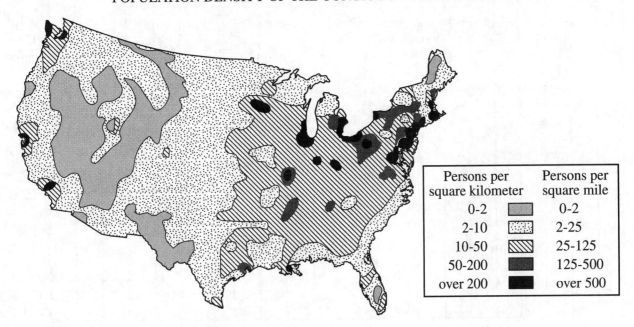

53. According to the information in the map above, which of the following statements is true for the 48 contiguous United States shown?

(A) The population of the United States is evenly distributed over the land.

(B) The Pacific coast of the United States is more densely populated than the Atlantic coast.

(C) The interior western states are the most sparsely populated in the United States.

(D) The southwestern region of the United States is more densely populated than the northeastern region.

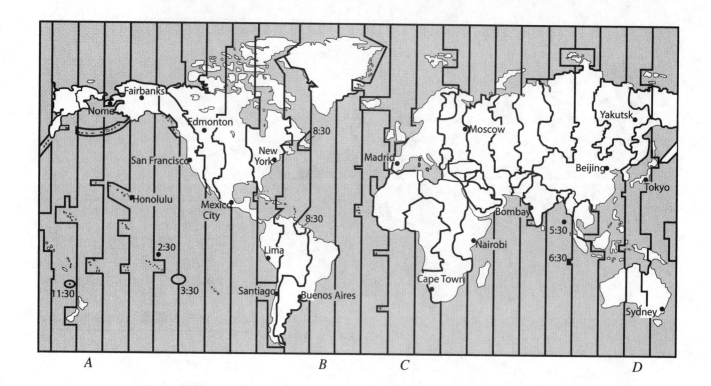

54. In which of the labeled time zones is the prime meridian located?

(A)   *A*
(B)   *B*
(C)   *C*
(D)   *D*

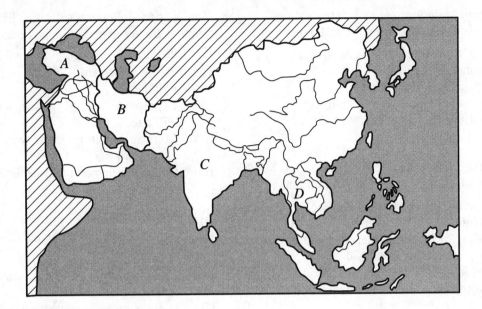

55. Buddhism is the predominant religion in which of the areas labeled on the map above?

   (A)   *A*
   (B)   *B*
   (C)   *C*
   (D)   *D*

56. An equatorial rain forest is associated with which of the following climatic conditions?

    (A) Cold, dry winters and warm, moist summers
    (B) Hot and wet year-round
    (C) Hot, sultry summers and mild winters
    (D) Cold, snowy winters and hot, dry summers

57. Which of the following is a power exercised by the Federal Reserve Bank of the United States?

    (A) Selecting the secretary of the Treasury
    (B) Auditing the budgets of the 50 states
    (C) Raising or lowering interest rates to fight inflation or a recession
    (D) Creating the budget for the federal government to be voted on by Congress

58. Which of the following will most likely occur when a country experiences an economic recession?

    (A) Tax revenues will increase and deficits will decline.
    (B) Exports will exceed imports and profits will rise.
    (C) Companies will hire new workers and wages will rise.
    (D) Consumer demand will decline and unemployment will rise.

59. According to supporters of international free-trade agreements, these agreements have the advantage of

    (A) creating a source of tax revenue through the collection of tariffs
    (B) aiding nations in protecting home industries and encouraging exports
    (C) increasing total world output while discouraging trade wars
    (D) protecting valuable natural resources from exportation to other countries

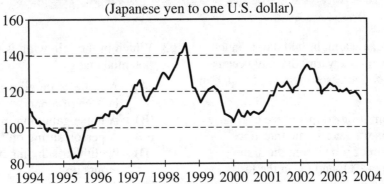

JAPAN/UNITED STATES FOREIGN EXCHANGE RATE
(Japanese yen to one U.S. dollar)

60. According to the chart above, in which of the following years would United States consumers have likely found it to their greatest economic advantage to buy goods made in Japan?

(A)   1995
(B)   1998
(C)   2000
(D)   2001

SCIENCE

61. For many people, a warm, humid day is much less comfortable than a warm, dry day because the high humidity decreases the rate of which of the following?

   (A)   Circulation of blood in surface capillaries
   (B)   Absorption of water in the intestines
   (C)   Evaporation of water from the skin
   (D)   Exchange of CO_2 and O_2 in the lungs

62. A young sailor watched sailing ships at sea and noted that they always appear to be "sinking" as they move away. Which of the following statements best explains the sailor's observation?

   (A)   Earth is orbiting the Sun.
   (B)   The Moon changes the tides.
   (C)   Earth is rotating.
   (D)   The surface of the ocean is curved.

63. Which of the following is the best example of potential energy?

   (A)   A turtle swimming slowly along the bottom of a pond
   (B)   A horse galloping in a race
   (C)   A person sitting on the beach
   (D)   A climber standing at the top of a tall mountain

64. In order to answer the question of whether mass is conserved during a chemical reaction in which a gas and a solid are produced, a student will need to measure which of the following?

   (A)   Pressure in the reaction container
   (B)   Weight of the products and reactants
   (C)   Volume of the product
   (D)   Reaction temperature

NET PRIMARY PRODUCTIVITY OF SELECTED ECOSYSTEMS
(grams/meter^2/year)

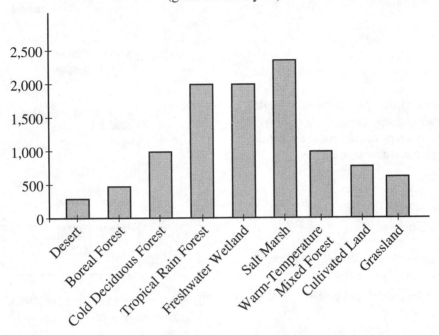

65. The graph above shows the levels of primary productivity (grams/meter^2/year) for different ecosystems. Which of the following can be concluded from the graph?

(A)　Primary productivity is highest in ecosystems with the largest numbers of animals.

(B)　Salt marshes contain the largest number of organisms.

(C)　Abundance of water is important to achieve high primary productivity levels.

(D)　The tropical rain forest and freshwater wetlands have similar numbers of plant species.

66. If a 6-inch bar magnet is cut crosswise into three equal pieces, what is the total number of magnetic poles among the three pieces?

(A) Two
(B) Three
(C) Four
(D) Six

67. A student has recorded the height of a single plant every day over the course of a year. Which of the following graphs is the most appropriate way to present the student's data?

(A) Bar graph
(B) Pie graph
(C) Line graph
(D) Multiple-line graph

68. Which of the following is true about lines of latitude?

(A) They circle Earth in an east-west direction.
(B) The prime meridian is a line of latitude.
(C) Lines of latitude are not parallel to each other.
(D) Lines of latitude separate Earth into different time zones.

69. Energy is transferred between individuals through a food web. In such a web, the producer organisms would be most likely to

(A) contain chlorophyll
(B) produce hemoglobin
(C) be decomposers
(D) be consumed by predators

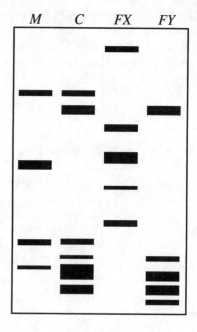

70. All humans have areas of DNA that are similar and areas of DNA that differ from person to person. Each person's DNA is a combination of the father's DNA and the mother's DNA. The figure above shows the DNA fingerprints of samples taken from four different individuals.

A mother (*M*) has given birth to a child (*C*) whose father is one of two men (*FX* and *FY*). Based on the separated samples of DNA shown above, which of the following is a correct statement about the father of *C* ?

(A) *FX* is the father.
(B) *FY* is the father.
(C) It is possible for either *FX* or *FY* to be the father.
(D) Neither *FX* nor *FY* could be the father.

71. When rabbits were artificially introduced to Australia, they rapidly multiplied because they had no natural predator. Overpopulating the area, the rabbits removed much of the grass, destroying the existing ecosystem. Which of the following is best illustrated by this example?

    (A) The importance of balance in an ecosystem
    (B) The loss of food energy at each trophic level in the ecosystem
    (C) The inability of the Australian environment to support grasslands
    (D) The poor ecological efficiency of ecosystems

72. The white feathers of the white-tailed ptarmigan in winter plumage make it nearly invisible against its snowy surroundings. This is an example of

    (A) sexual reproduction
    (B) homeostasis
    (C) ecological succession
    (D) evolutionary adaptation

73. Earth's 24-hour solar day is caused by

    (A) Earth's revolution around the Sun
    (B) the Moon's revolution around Earth
    (C) Earth's rotation on its axis
    (D) the Moon's rotation on its axis

74. Which of the following is most likely the reason that many groups lobby Congress to secure the preservation of forests?

    (A) Many pharmaceuticals contain active ingredients first discovered in plant species found growing wild in forests.
    (B) Forests shade the ground and limit the growth of small shrubs, which decreases diversity.
    (C) Forests produce high amounts of carbon dioxide, which is necessary to support life.
    (D) The removal of forests increases the chances of uncontrollable fires.

Questions 75–76 refer to the following information.

Peppered moths exist in two colors, light and dark, as shown in the figures above. Around the middle of the nineteenth century, few of the dark forms were seen in the woods of England. But as industrialization swept the country, the frequency of black moths increased a hundredfold, while the light form nearly disappeared. Scientists have theorized that this was due to the blackening of their habitat from increased air pollution.

75. Which of the following mechanisms can best explain the change in the moth population?

    (A)   Artificial selection
    (B)   Natural selection
    (C)   Migration
    (D)   Speciation

76. Which of the following scientists' work would best explain the information above?

    (A)   Charles Darwin
    (B)   Gregor Mendel
    (C)   Watson and Crick
    (D)   Robert Hooke

Questions 77–78 refer to the following information.

The graph below represents carbon monoxide emissions from various sources in the United States between 1986 and 1995.

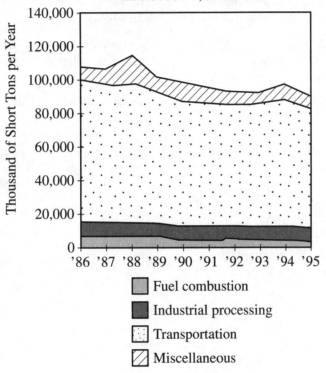

U.S. CARBON MONOXIDE
EMISSIONS, 1986-1995

■ Fuel combustion

■ Industrial processing

▫ Transportation

▨ Miscellaneous

77. Which of the following caused the greatest amount of carbon monoxide emissions during the time period shown in the graph?

(A) Fuel combustion
(B) Industrial processing
(C) Transportation
(D) Miscellaneous

78. What can be concluded about the level of carbon monoxide emissions in the United States in 2003 if the following three statements are true?

I. More cars were driven in 2003 than in 1995.
II. Newer cars emit less carbon monoxide than older cars.
III. Emissions due to fuel combustion, industrial processing, and miscellaneous sources remained constant.

(A) Carbon monoxide emissions are the same as in 1995.
(B) Carbon monoxide emissions are lower than in 1995.
(C) Carbon monoxide emissions are higher than in 1995.
(D) There is not enough information to determine the relative amount of carbon monoxide emissions.

Questions 79–80 refer to the following information.

Natasha has a small stone. She fills a large beaker to the top with water and places a smaller beaker below the spout of the larger beaker. Natasha drops the stone into the larger beaker and it sinks to the bottom. She then measures the water that spills into the smaller beaker, using a graduated cylinder.

79. What property of the stone does Natasha want to measure?

   (A)   Mass
   (B)   Volume
   (C)   Conductivity
   (D)   Buoyancy

80. What conclusion can Natasha draw about the density of the stone?

   (A)   The stone is less dense than the water.
   (B)   The stone is equal in density to the water.
   (C)   The stone is greater in density than the water.
   (D)   The density depends on the starting volume of water in the larger beaker.

Chapter 6
Right Answers and Explanations for the Practice Questions

▶ ▶ ▶ ▶ ▶ ▶ ▶ ▶ ▶ ▶ ▶ ▶

Right Answers and Explanations for the Practice Questions

Now that you have answered all of the practice questions, you can check your work. Compare your answers with the correct answers in the table below.

Question Number	Correct Answer	Content Category
1	C	Literary Methods and Effects
2	A	Reading Literature
3	D	Literary Methods and Effects
4	D	Literary Methods and Effects
5	A	Literary Methods and Effects
6	C	Reading Literature
7	B	Literary Methods and Effects
8	C	Reading Literature
9	B	Literary Methods and Effects
10	A	Reading Literature
11	A	Reading Literature
12	A	Reading Literature
13	B	Literary Methods and Effects
14	B	Reading and Communication Skills
15	B	Reading and Communication Skills
16	B	Reading and Communication Skills
17	A	Reading and Communication Skills
18	C	Reading and Communication Skills
19	D	Reading and Communication Skills
20	C	Reading and Communication Skills
21	B	Number Sense and Basic Algebra
22	A	Geometry & Measurement
23	B	Geometry & Measurement
24	A	Number Sense and Basic Algebra
25	A	Geometry & Measurement
26	B	Data Analysis & Probability
27	C	Number Sense and Basic Algebra
28	D	Number Sense and Basic Algebra
29	B	Data Analysis & Probability
30	A	Number Sense and Basic Algebra
31	D	Number Sense and Basic Algebra
32	D	Geometry & Measurement
33	D	Number Sense and Basic Algebra
34	C	Number Sense and Basic Algebra
35	A	Number Sense and Basic Algebra
36	D	Data Analysis & Probability
37	C	Data Analysis & Probability
38	B	Data Analysis & Probability
39	B	Geometry & Measurement
40	B	Geometry & Measurement
41	B	Historical Continuity and Change
42	B	Historical Continuity and Change
43	C	Historical Continuity and Change
44	C	Historical Continuity and Change
45	D	Historical Continuity and Change
46	A	Historical Continuity and Change

Question Number	Correct Answer	Content Category
47	B	Historical Continuity and Change
48	B	Historical Continuity and Change
49	B	Civics and Government
50	C	Civics and Government
51	B	Civics and Government
52	C	Civics and Government
53	C	People, Places, and Geographic Regions
54	C	People, Places, and Geographic Regions
55	D	People, Places, and Geographic Regions
56	B	People, Places, and Geographic Regions
57	C	Scarcity and Economic Choice
58	D	Scarcity and Economic Choice
59	C	Scarcity and Economic Choice
60	B	Scarcity and Economic Choice
61	C	Basic Principles and Fundamentals of Science
62	D	Nature and History of Science
63	D	Basic Principles and Fundamentals of Science
64	B	Nature and History of Science
65	C	Basic Principles and Fundamentals of Science
66	D	Basic Principles and Fundamentals of Science
67	C	Nature and History of Science
68	A	Basic Principles and Fundamentals of Science
69	A	Basic Principles and Fundamentals of Science
70	B	Science/Technology and Social Perspectives
71	A	Basic Principles and Fundamentals of Science
72	D	Basic Principles and Fundamentals of Science
73	C	Basic Principles and Fundamentals of Science
74	A	Science/Technology and Social Perspectives
75	B	Basic Principles and Fundamentals of Science
76	A	Nature and History of Science
77	C	Nature and History of Science
78	D	Nature and History of Science
79	B	Basic Principles and Fundamentals of Science
80	C	Nature and History of Science

Explanations of Right Answers

ENGLISH LANGUAGE ARTS

1. This question tests your ability to understand the content of a passage. According to the passage, anyone seeing the snow that had fallen in the narrator's town would know why people in the town love stories so much. By describing the snowy scene and indicating that its beauty made people feel "that anything could happen," the narrator suggests a feeling of unlimited possibility. Thus, the best answer is (C).

2. This question tests your ability to understand and compare two poems. In the first poem, the following phrases are used to describe the fog: "on little cat feet," "It sits looking," and "on silent haunches." In the second poem, such phrases as "rubs its back," "rubs its muzzle," and "Licked its tongue" are used to describe the fog. Since each of these phrases could be used to describe an animal, the best answer is (A).

3. This question tests your ability to interpret the content of a poem. The last line of the poem, "Curled once about the house, and fell asleep," suggests that the fog will linger about the house all night. Thus, the best answer is (D).

4. This question tests your ability to identify the way in which an author develops a character. In the excerpt, the speaker describes what he learned from Ultima: the names of plants and animals, and an ability to appreciate nature. Thus, the best answer is (D).

5. This question tests your ability to understand the tone of a poem. In the poem, the speaker describes a state of sadness that results from "thinking of the days that are no more" (line 5). Nostalgia is a longing for things, persons, or situations of the past. Thus, the best answer is (A).

6. This question tests your ability to understand the meaning of a phrase used in the context of a poem. According to the poet, his tears arise from despair, or complete loss of hope—a very strong feeling. Describing his despair as being divine and having depths further emphasizes the intensity of the emotion he feels. Therefore, the best answer is (C). There is no mention in the poem of another's unhappiness or of divine retribution, or punishment, so (A) and (D) are not correct. The poet does not indicate that he has done anything wrong, so (B) is also incorrect.

7. This question tests your ability to understand the way in which an author uses particular details to portray a setting. The author's assertion that "something is wrong with the month of May" in the town of Verity is followed by illustrative examples. When the sea turtles begin migrating across West Main Street, odd things happen: girls and babies behave in a distressed manner and ficus hedges burst into flame. These details suggest that Verity in May is "strange and distressing." Thus, the best answer is (B). Although some of the details could be seen as making Verity dangerous, there is no indication in the passage that the town is beautiful, as in (C). There is no indication in the passage that Verity is isolated and lonely, (A), nor that it is the new growth of spring that is affecting the town, (D).

8. This question tests your ability to identify the primary concern of a passage as a whole. The passage describes the children going up the street and turning into the school court and also mentions the topics of which they spoke as they went. Therefore, the best answer is (C). It is clear that the children were not yet in the classroom, so (A) is not correct. Feelings about families are not among the topics mentioned, and there is no indication in the passage that the children are playing a game, so (B) and (D) are also incorrect.

9. This question tests your ability to understand the content of a passage. The narrator states that the children passed run-down apartment buildings where residents have difficult lives, but the children "did not trouble themselves about these." Instead they spoke about a variety of topics that were of interest to them. Thus, the best answer is (B). No mention is made in the passage of a particular school event, so (A) is incorrect. Since the children are talking together, it is unlikely that they are unfriendly toward each other, and there is no indication that they are reluctant to get to school, so (C) and (D) are also incorrect.

10. This question tests your ability to identify the relationship between elements in a passage. The words "Bits of pink, of blue, white, yellow, green, purple, brown, black" describe the children's clothing, a contrast with "the unhandsome gray and decay of the double-apartment buildings." Thus, the best answer is (A). Since the children's concerns are wide-ranging rather than narrow, (B) is incorrect. No mention is made of the school's discipline or of the children's teachers, so (C) and (D) are incorrect.

11. This question tests your ability to identify the primary concern of a passage. The author describes the importance of music in a character's life. This character believed that "life, true life, was something that was stored in music." Further, the records he cherished and the live performances he was able to see are "the marks by which he gauged his ability to love." Love of music is clearly an important aspect of his personality. Thus, the best answer is (A). (B) is incorrect because the passage does not discuss more than one character in detail. (C) and (D) are incorrect because the passage focuses on the character's love for music, not on how that love came about or what it led to.

12. This question tests your ability to draw an inference about a character. The best answer is (A). According to the passage, the character measured his ability to love in terms of his opportunities to listen to music. In contrast, his family and his work did not provide such a measure. Thus, it can be inferred that music provided greater emotional satisfaction than did his work or his family.

13. This question tests your ability to understand the content of a passage. The character is described as someone who "worked harder than anyone." Thus, the best answer is (B).

14. This question tests your ability to identify an author's primary purpose. The best answer is (B). The author explores the way graffiti in his neighborhood looks, the surprising places where it occurs, and its mysterious origins. His observation that, "Amazingly," graffiti appears though no one is seen creating it indicates his wonder at the graffiti's occurrence. Thus, the correct answer is (B). (C) is incorrect because the author indicates that he does not know what techniques graffiti artists use. (A) and (D) are incorrect because the author simply describes the graffiti; he does not pass judgment on whether it should exist.

15. This question tests your ability to understand the way in which an author portrays a character. In the passage, the narrator primarily describes her mother in terms of how much her mother is able to accomplish in spite of certain obstacles. The mother's character—her "iron will and great powers of endurance"—is revealed through her ability to perform the arduous daily work necessary to care for her home and family. Thus, the best answer is (B).

16. This question tests your ability to identify the attitude of the author toward a character. The author's description of her mother's arduous daily routine is followed by the phrase "But she was no quitter." This phrase reflects her mother's ability to persevere in accomplishing her many tasks in spite of the difficult conditions she faced. The author clearly admires her mother's ability to cope with the difficulties in her life. Thus, the best answer is (B).

17. This question tests your ability to understand the function of a particular element in a passage. The author states that her mother did not neglect any "standard of cleanliness or nicety of domestic arrangements" in spite of the lack of modern conveniences, limited supply of water, and "the never-ending red dust," examples of the obstacles that her mother was able to overcome. Thus, the best answer is (A). There is no indication in the passage that the author's mother was endangered by her way of life or that her efforts were futile, so (B) and (D) are incorrect. The red dust is not relevant to the way in which the author's mother might have gained her powers of endurance, so (C) is also incorrect.

18. This question tests your ability to identify the intended audience for a particular passage. Since the author begins the passage by giving advice to someone who might "want to be a serious writer," the best answer is (C).

19. This question tests your ability to draw a conclusion about the meaning of a word in the context of a passage. In line 4, the author refers to "illogical systems" that budding writers use to record their thoughts and ideas. In lines 5-6, the author provides an example of such an illogical system: "the messy process of jotting hasty notes on any available" piece of paper. Clearly the author does not find this "process" to be effective. Thus (D) is the best answer.

20. The question tests your ability to edit a passage (in order to clarify its meaning). By stating "My plan was new," the author indicates that her solo journey to the magnetic North Pole is different from past expeditions. Only (C) serves to emphasize the difference between two ideas.

MATHEMATICS

21. Since the answer choices are sufficiently far apart, you can determine the one that is the closest estimate by using the following estimates for the four charges.

$212.56 ≈ $210
$56.41 ≈ $60
$5.17 ≈ $5
$10.74 ≈ $10

The total of the four estimates is $210 + $60 + $5 + $10 = $285. Thus, the closest estimate of Lin's total charges is $285. The correct answer is (B).

22. According to Erica's class schedule, period 2 begins at 9:52 and ends at 11:14. To find how many minutes there are between 9:52 and 11:14, you can use the fact that there are 60 minutes in 1 hour and split up the time period as follows.

From 9:52 to 10:00 is 8 minutes.
From 10:00 to 11:00 is 60 minutes.
From 11:00 to 11:14 is 14 minutes.

Thus, to find how many minutes long period 2 is, add these three numbers of minutes.

8 minutes + 60 minutes + 14 minutes = 82 minutes

The problem can also be solved by subtraction, but you must be careful when subtracting times because you cannot regroup in the usual way.

Hours	Minutes
10	74
~~11~~	~~14~~ (14 + 60 = 74)
−9	−52
1	22

Thus, the amount of time between 9:52 and 11:14 is 1 hour 22 minutes, or 82 minutes. The correct answer is (A).

23. Erica's school day starts at 8:05 A.M. and ends at 2:40 P.M. The total amount of time from 8:05 A.M. to 2:40 P.M. is equal to the amount of time from 8:05 A.M. to 12:05 P.M., or 4 hours, plus the amount of time from 12:05 P.M. to 2:40 P.M., or 2 hours 35 minutes.

Thus, the total amount of time from 8:05 A.M. to 2:40 P.M. is equal to

4 hours + 2 hours + 35 minutes = 6 hours 35 minutes

To convert 35 minutes to a fraction of an hour, divide 35 by 60, since there are 60 minutes in 1 hour. The result is $\frac{35}{60} = \frac{7}{12}$.

Thus, Erica's school day is $6\frac{7}{12}$ hours long. The correct answer is (B).

24. It is given that a cup of whole milk has 30 more calories than a cup of orange juice. If j represents the number of calories in a cup of orange juice, then 30 more than j can be expressed as $j + 30$. Thus, in terms of j, the number of calories in a cup of whole milk can be represented by $j + 30$. The correct answer is (A).

25. To find the number of hours that the plumber worked last Saturday, first find the amount that the plumber charged for work last Friday. The amount that the plumber charged for the hours worked last Friday is obtained by multiplying the number of hours worked, 4, by the hourly rate charged for Friday, $36.

    Amount charged Friday $= 4 \times \$36 = \$144$

    To find the amount that the plumber charged for the hours worked last Saturday, subtract $144 (the charge for Friday) from $288 (the total charge for the job). The result is $\$288 - \$144 = \$144$.

    You can now find the number of hours that the plumber worked last Saturday by dividing the amount charged last Saturday, $144, by the hourly rate charged for Saturday, $48. Thus, the number of hours is $\dfrac{\$144}{\$48} = 3$. The correct answer is (A).

26. In order to solve this problem, it may be helpful to use the definition of average (arithmetic mean). Given a set of test grades for a class, the class average is equal to the sum of the grades divided by the number of grades.

    $$\text{class average} = \frac{\text{the sum of the grades}}{\text{the number of grades}}$$

    According to this definition, to find the sum of the grades, multiply the class average by the number of grades. Let n denote the number of students who originally took the test. Then, the sum of the grades in Mr. Shaw's class that averaged 75 is $75 \times n$. Therefore, the sum of these grades plus the new grade of 85 can be expressed as $(75 \times n) + 85$, and so the new class average is given by $\dfrac{(75 \times n) + 85}{n + 1}$.

    By writing 85 as $75 + 10$, the new class average can be expressed as

    $$\frac{(75 \times n) + 75 + 10}{n + 1} = \frac{75 \times (n + 1) + 10}{n + 1} = \frac{75 \times (n + 1)}{n + 1} + \frac{10}{n + 1} = 75 + \frac{10}{n + 1}.$$

    Note that since $n + 1$ represents an integer greater than 1, the fraction $\dfrac{10}{n + 1}$ is a number less than 10. Thus, the new class average must be less than 10 points higher than before. The correct answer is (B).

27. According to the table, each basket must contain 3 oranges. Since Mrs. Graham has 53 oranges, to find the number of baskets that she can assemble, divide 53 by 3.

$$\text{number of baskets } = \frac{53}{3} = 17\frac{2}{3}$$

Since she cannot assemble a fraction of a basket, the greatest number of baskets that she can assemble is 17.

The number of candies that would be required for these baskets can be found by multiplying the greatest number of baskets (17) by the number of candies per basket (8). Thus, the number of candies required is $17 \times 8 = 136$. The correct answer is (C).

28. According to the list of ingredients, $5\frac{1}{4}$ cups of fish stock are needed to make 4 servings. In a recipe, the number of servings is proportional to the amount of each ingredient. For example, doubling the amount of each ingredient would double the number of servings that can be made. Thus, to find the number of cups of fish stock needed to make 6 servings, set up a proportion:

$$\frac{\text{number of servings}}{\text{number of cups of fish stock}} = \frac{4}{5\frac{1}{4}} = \frac{6}{\text{number of cups of fish stock}}$$

This proportion can be solved by cross multiplying:

4 times the number of cups of fish stock is equal to $6 \times 5\frac{1}{4}$; the number of cups of fish stock needed

for 6 servings is $\frac{1}{4} \times 6 \times 5\frac{1}{4} = \frac{1}{4} \times 6 \times \frac{21}{4} = \frac{6 \times 21}{4 \times 4} = \frac{126}{16} = 7\frac{14}{16} = 7\frac{7}{8}$.

Thus, $7\frac{7}{8}$ cups of fish stock are needed to make 6 servings of the dinner. The correct answer is (D).

29. According to the table, there are 75 blue balls and 50 white balls in the container. Thus, the number of balls that are either blue or white is $75 + 50 = 125$.

The probability that the ball selected will be either blue or white is equal to the fraction of the total number of balls in the container that are either blue or white; that is, the probability is equal to

$$\frac{\text{number of blue balls } + \text{ number of white balls}}{\text{total number of balls}} = \frac{125}{500} = \frac{25}{100} = \frac{1}{4}.$$

Thus, the probability that the selected ball will be either blue or white is $\frac{1}{4}$. The correct answer is (B).

30. The percent of the 1,500 people who were younger than 36 years old can be found by subtracting 62% from 100%, since 100% represents all 1,500 people and 62% represents those who were 36 years old or older.

    Percent younger than 36 years old = 100% − 62% = 38%

    To find the actual number of people who were younger than 36 years old, express 38% as a decimal and multiply 1,500 by that decimal.

    $0.38 \times 1,500 = 570$

    Thus, 570 people who renewed their driver's licenses were younger than 36 years old. The correct answer is (A).

31. In order to compare the four annual budgets given in the table, it may be helpful first to change the budget amounts for City A and City D, which are in billions of dollars, to equivalent amounts in millions of dollars, using the definition of billion that is given.

    1 million = 1,000,000
    1 billion = 1,000,000,000 = 1,000 million

    Thus, to change $0.224 billion to an amount in millions of dollars, multiply 0.224 by 1,000 by moving the decimal point in 0.224 three places to the right.

    $0.224 billion = $0.224 × 1,000 million = $224 million

    Similarly, $0.216 billion = $0.216 × 1,000 million = $216 million.

    Thus, the budgets of City A, City B, City C, and City D are $224 million, $226.5 million, $218.9 million, and $216 million, respectively. City D, therefore, has the smallest budget. The correct answer is (D).

32. It is given that $\frac{1}{2}$ inch on the map corresponds to an actual distance of 5 miles, so 1 inch on the map represents an actual distance of 10 miles.

    Thus, $1\frac{1}{2}$ inches on the map represents an actual distance of $1\frac{1}{2} \times 10 = 15$ miles, and 4 inches on the map represents an actual distance of $4 \times 10 = 40$ miles.

    Thus, a rectangular region on the map measuring $1\frac{1}{2}$ inches by 4 inches represents an actual rectangular region measuring 15 miles by 40 miles.

    To find the actual area, in square miles, multiply the two dimensions, 15 miles and 40 miles. The actual area is 15 miles × 40 miles = 600 square miles. The correct answer is (D).

33. One way to find the value of *x* is to set up an equation in *x* that represents Bob's checking account balance before and after the indicated transactions, keeping in mind that a deposit must be added to the account balance and an amount taken out must be subtracted from the account balance.

    Thus, to the balance of $982, *x* dollars must be added, and then $35 dollars must be subtracted, resulting in a new balance of $1,104. The relationship between the old balance and the new balance can be expressed by the following equation.

    $$982 + x - 35 = 1,104$$

    Subtracting 35 from 982 equals 947, so the equation becomes $947 + x = 1,104$. The value of *x*, therefore, is $1,104 - 947 = 157$. The correct answer is (D).

34. It is given that the ratio of the number of male students to the number of female students is 5 to 7. This means that for every 7 female students in the school, there are 5 male students, or that for every 12 students in the school, 5 are male students. Therefore, $\frac{5}{12}$ of the students are males.

    The total number of students in the school is 600. To find how many are male students, multiply 600 by $\frac{5}{12}$, which is 250. The correct answer is (C).

35. According to the table, the trip began in New York at 2:32 P.M. (New York local time) and ended in Los Angeles at 5:46 P.M. (Los Angeles local time).

    To find the total time for the trip, you need to find the total amount of time that elapsed between 2:32 P.M., New York time, and 5:46 P.M., Los Angeles time.

    You cannot simply subtract the time 2:32 P.M. from the time 5:46 P.M., however, since the two times represent times in different time zones. You must take into account that local time in Los Angeles is $2 + 1 = 3$ hours earlier than local time in New York. This means, for example, that when it is 7 P.M. in New York, it is 4 P.M. in Los Angeles.

    So when the trip ended in Los Angeles at 5:46 P.M. local time, it was 8:46 P.M. local time in New York. Therefore, to find the total time for the trip, subtract 2 hours 32 minutes from 8 hours 46 minutes.

    $$\begin{array}{r} 8 \text{ hr } 46 \text{ min} \\ -2 \text{ hr } 32 \text{ min} \\ \hline 6 \text{ hr } 14 \text{ min} \end{array}$$

    The correct answer is (A).

36. According to the table, the probability that the pigeon will peck the button in the experiment is 0.80. This means that for every 100 times that the experiment is repeated, the pigeon will peck the button 80 times; 20 times out of 100 the pigeon will <u>not</u> peck the button. Since 20 out of 100 is $\frac{20}{100} = 20\%$, the pigeon will <u>not</u> peck the button 20% of the times that the experiment is repeated.

Thus, if the experiment is repeated 40 times, the expected number of times that the pigeon will <u>not</u> peck the button can be found by multiplying 40 by the decimal equivalent of 20%.

$$20\% \text{ of } 40 = 0.2 \times 40 = 8$$

Thus, the expected number of times that the pigeon will <u>not</u> peck the button is 8. The correct answer is (D).

37. According to the circle graph, Gail spends 55% of the 10 hours that she spends in school each day in classes and 20% of the 10 hours in extracurricular activities. Thus, Gail spends 55% − 20% = 35% more hours in classes than in extracurricular activities.

To find how many hours this is, convert 35% to the decimal 0.35 and multiply 10 by this decimal.

$$0.35 \times 10 \text{ hours} = 3.5 \text{ hours} = 3\frac{1}{2} \text{ hours}$$

Thus, Gail spends $3\frac{1}{2}$ more hours in classes than in extracurricular activities. The correct answer is (C).

38. According to the circle graph, Gail spends 15% of the time that she spends at school each day in study hall. Since percent means "per 100," to convert 15% to a fraction, write the fraction with numerator 15 and denominator 100, and reduce the fraction to lowest terms.

$$15\% = \frac{15}{100} = \frac{3}{20}$$

Thus, $\frac{3}{20}$ of the time Gail spends at school is spent in study hall. The correct answer is (B).

39. The perimeter of a rectangular room is the sum of the lengths of the four sides of the room. According to the table, the dimensions of the family room are 24 feet by 18 feet. Thus, the perimeter of the family room is equal to

$$24 \text{ ft} + 18 \text{ ft} + 24 \text{ ft} + 18 \text{ ft} = 84 \text{ ft}.$$

Similarly, the perimeter of the living room is equal to

$$20 \text{ ft} + 16 \text{ ft} + 20 \text{ ft} + 16 \text{ ft} = 72 \text{ ft}.$$

To find how much greater the perimeter of the family room is than the perimeter of the living room, subtract 72 ft from 84 ft. The result is 84 ft − 72 ft = 12 ft. The correct answer is (B).

40. To find the total cost of the carpeting needed to cover the family room, you need to find the area of the family room. Note that you must find the area in square yards, since you are given the cost per square yard for carpeting. Therefore, you first have to convert the family room's dimensions, 24 ft and 18 ft, to yards.

   To convert 24 ft to yards, divide 24 by 3, since 1 yard = 3 feet. So 24 ft = $\frac{24}{3}$ yards = 8 yards. Similarly, 18 ft = $\frac{18}{3}$ yards = 6 yards. Thus, the dimensions of the family room, in yards, are 8 yards by 6 yards.

   To find the area of the family room, recall that the area of a rectangle is the product of its two dimensions. The area of the family room is 8 yards × 6 yards = 48 square yards.

   You can now find the cost of the carpeting by multiplying 48 (the number of square yards of carpeting needed) by $20 (the cost per square yard). The cost is 48 × $20 = $960. The correct answer is (B).

CITIZENSHIP AND SOCIAL SCIENCE

41. This question uses a map to test your ability to identify a chronological time period in the history of the United States. The map shows the eastern seaboard of the United States with political boundaries for the thirteen colonies and the Proclamation Line of 1763. The line was one of the early issues leading to conflict between the British government and the American colonists. The correct answer, therefore, is (B).

42. This question tests your knowledge of the issues and problems that contributed to the coming of the American Revolution. Following the French and Indian War, the British government passed a series of tax laws in an attempt to pay the debt incurred by fighting the French in North America. The North American colonists did not have any elected representatives in Parliament to present their case for opposing these tax laws, such as the Stamp Act and Townshend duties. The colonists protested this "taxation without representation." The correct answer, therefore, is (B).

43. This question tests your knowledge of the continental expansion of the United States. Shortly after purchasing the Louisiana Territory from France in 1803, President Thomas Jefferson selected Meriwether Lewis, his personal secretary and a captain in the army, and William Clark, Lewis' lieutenant, to travel westward to explore the flora and fauna of the Louisiana territory and search for a waterway to the Pacific Ocean. The correct answer, therefore, is (C).

44. This question tests your knowledge of the Constitutional Convention and the method by which one of the compromises was reached to bring about its adoption. Opponents of the new United States Constitution feared the new government would use its powers to deny the rights of individual citizens. In exchange for support of the Constitution, these opponents demanded that a series of amendments be added to the Constitution to guarantee the rights of individuals. These ten amendments are the Bill of Rights (1791). The correct answer, therefore, is (C).

45. This question tests your knowledge of the causes of the French Revolution. There was a series of causes leading to the revolution, including adoption of some of the political ideals of the American Revolution, poor harvests leading to inflation, and an increase in the price of bread, a staple of the French peasant diet. Foreign adventures in Europe and abroad, such as support for the American Revolution, had run up the French national debt. The correct answer, therefore, is (D).

46. This question tests your ability to interpret a graph. The graph illustrates the percent breakdown of key resources between northern and southern states. Northern resources are read from the left and shown in the white bars. The gray bars illustrate southern resources. The human and capital resources necessary to produce war weaponry in the northern states exceeded the resources of the southern states. The correct answer, therefore, is (A).

47. This question tests your ability to distinguish between statements of fact and opinion. All three of the statements made in choices (A), (C), and (D) are supported as statements based on factual evidence of events that occurred. Most historians believe that the Treaty of Versailles was a major contributing factor to German acceptance of Nazism, but it is an opinion of historians rather than a statement of fact. The correct answer, therefore, is (B).

48. This question tests your knowledge of the roles played by key individuals in the twentieth century. Each of the women listed in the group was the political leader of her country in the post-Second World War period. Indira Gandhi was prime minister of India. Golda Meir was prime minister of Israel. Margaret Thatcher was prime minister of the United Kingdom. The correct answer, therefore, is (B).

49. This question tests your knowledge of the distribution of powers between the national government and state governments in a federal system. Raising an army and a navy, (A), and imposing tariffs on imported goods, (D), are expressed powers of the national government. Issuing driver's licenses, (C), is a power reserved to the states. Levying taxes on income is a power, like borrowing money or establishing courts, that is concurrent, or shared by the two levels of government. The correct answer, therefore, is (B).

50. This question tests your knowledge of the rights and responsibilities of citizens. Citizens are called by the federal, state, and local governments across the United States to serve as jurors in cases in their respective jurisdictions. Individuals called for jury duty may or may not actually serve on a jury depending upon the outcome of the jury-selection process. This service is commonly referred to as "jury duty." The correct answer, therefore, is (C).

51. This question tests your understanding of the system of checks and balances that are a part of the functioning of the United States Constitution. In the case of *Marbury* v. *Madison* in 1803, the Supreme Court secured the power of judicial review of acts of Congress. The Congress may, however, by a two-thirds vote of each house, and with the agreement of three-fourths of the states, amend the Constitution to overcome a decision of the Supreme Court. The correct answer, therefore, is (B).

52. This question tests your knowledge of the functions of the United Nations. The United Nations seeks to carry out policies and programs to promote peaceful solutions to conflicts within nations and among nations and to administer humanitarian programs. It authorized the use of military force in Korea following the North Korean invasion of South Korea in 1950. It has subsequently passed other resolutions to authorize the use of force to check acts of aggression. The correct answer, therefore, is (C).

53. This question tests your ability to interpret graphic information about the distribution of population on a map. The scale in the box illustrates that the population density of the United States is sparsest in the interior western states, including the Rocky Mountains and adjoining territory. The correct answer, therefore, is (C).

54. This question tests your knowledge of the location of a key place on the globe. The Earth is divided into 24 time zones. The base time is set at the prime meridian, which passes through the Royal Observatory at Greenwich, England, and is referred to as Greenwich mean time (GMT). The correct answer, therefore, is (C).

55. This question tests your knowledge of the distribution of major religions in Asia. Buddhism was founded in the sixth century B.C.E. in northern India. As early as the fourth century C.E., it began to decline in India and moved to eastern and southern Asian countries, including China, Korea, Japan, and Thailand. The correct answer, therefore, is (D).

56. This question tests your knowledge of the characteristics of climate regions. Climate regions tend to be classified into categories in relation to their proximity to the equator or the polar areas. Equatorial rain forest or low-latitude climates receive the direct rays of the Sun year-round, making temperatures high, and they experience large amounts of rainfall and humidity. The correct answer, therefore, is (B).

57. This question tests your knowledge of the functions of the Federal Reserve Bank of the United States in influencing the direction of the United States economy. Two of the primary functions of the Federal Reserve are to create a stable banking system and money supply. In addition, the Federal Reserve uses monetary policy to stimulate the economy in times of recession by lowering interest rates and by conversely creating higher interest rates to limit rates of inflation to acceptable levels. The correct answer, therefore, is (C).

58. This question tests your understanding of the economic characteristics that are present in a recession. Generally, a recession is described as a slowdown in economic activity as measured by real output, normally the gross domestic product (GDP). Tax revenues decline as people earn less money or are laid off. Consumers spend less money (lower demand) because they are unemployed or fear becoming unemployed. Businesses need fewer workers (higher unemployment) because inventories are not as quickly depleted. The correct answer, therefore, is (D)

59. This question tests your knowledge of international economics. Advocates of international free-trade agreements base much of their argument on the efficiencies that exist when there is an absence of trade barriers. International free-trade agreements seek to increase total world or regional economic output by discouraging trade-war practices, such as tariffs, subsidies, and quotas. The correct answer, therefore, is (C).

60. This question tests your understanding of currency-exchange rates. The United States dollar and the Japanese yen float against one another. The exchange rate for the two currencies is constantly changing. The higher the number of Japanese yen that may be purchased for one United States dollar, the more the United States dollar will buy in goods made in Japan. During the year 1998, the United States dollar could buy between 125 and 145 Japanese yen. The correct answer, therefore, is (B).

SCIENCE

61. Water evaporates more slowly from the skin on a humid day because the air is approaching the saturation point with respect to water vapor. The evaporation of water has a cooling effect on the skin because the water absorbs heat energy from the skin to make the transition from the liquid to the vapor phase. With water evaporating more slowly on a humid day, there is less evaporative cooling and as a result, many people are less comfortable. The correct answer, therefore, is (C).

62. This question asks you develop a reasonable scientific explanation for a commonly observed natural phenomenon. As the boat moves away from the observer, it is moving over Earth's curved surface. As the distance increases, the curvature prevents the observer from seeing greater portions of the lower part of the boat, and so it appears that the boat is sinking. The answer, therefore, is (D).

63. This question requires a basic understanding of potential energy. Potential energy is the stored energy an object has due to its relative position to some other object. The examples provided as choices in the question include motion as well as position. The energy of motion is kinetic energy and is not part of the potential energy an object possesses. Choice (D) is the correct answer because the height of the object (climber) is greater than in any of the other examples provided.

64. This question asks you to select a scientific process that could be used to investigate a fundamental principle in chemistry: the law of conservation of mass. This law states that matter cannot be created or destroyed in a chemical reaction. The mass or weight of the reactants and products is the evidence that is needed to demonstrate this law; therefore, the correct answer is (B).

65. This question asks that graphical data be interpreted using ecological knowledge. Net primary productivity refers to the amount of organic matter that is produced by photosynthesis and that is available to support consumers and decomposers. Primary productivity does not provide information about the number of species of plants or their associated animal life. Based on the graph, the tropical rain forest, the freshwater wetland, and the salt marsh are the most productive ecosystems. These ecosystems also have the greatest amount of available water. The correct answer, therefore, is (C).

66. This question asks for an understanding of magnets. A north magnetic pole always exists with the presence of a south pole and vice versa. When a magnet is cut in half, each half still behaves as a complete magnet, so each half will have two poles. Cutting a magnet into three pieces will result in three smaller magnets, each with two poles. Therefore, a total of six poles are produced from the cutting of the original magnet. The correct answer is (D).

67. This question asks that you identify an appropriate graphic presentation of data. A line graph is most appropriate when tracking the trend of a single object. A bar graph is commonly used for illustrating values for categories or for discontinuous data. A pie chart (circle graph) is appropriate when the relative proportions or percentages of several subgroups are compared for a single larger category. A multiple-line graph is used for representing trends of several items. Since the data for a single item is to be displayed and the trend for the data is important, a line graph, choice (C), is the most appropriate graph.

68. This question requires knowledge of Earth Science. The equator has been designated as 0° latitude. Other lines of latitude are parallel to the equator, all circling Earth in an east-west direction. The correct answer, therefore, is (A).

69. This question asks about organisms in a food web with respect to their role in energy transformations and the chemical requirements to fulfill this role. Producer organisms are capable of using energy from the Sun to make glucose through the process of photosynthesis. Most photosynthetic organisms use chlorophyll to absorb the necessary sunlight. The correct answer, therefore, is (A).

70. This question requires knowledge of biotechnology and interpretation of a diagram of labeled DNA fragments that were separated by gel electrophoresis. Since the DNA of the child is a combination of parental DNA, each of the bands shown for the child must correspond to the bands shown for one or both parents. Based on the bands shown, only *FY* could be the father because there are several bands common between the DNA patterns for the child and *FY* whereas there are no DNA bands common between the child and *FX*. The correct answer, therefore, is (B).

71. This question requires an understanding the relationship between organisms and their environment. Predator-prey relationships play an important role in maintaining the balance of organisms in an ecosystem. Without a natural predator, the prey population would increase unchecked until the resources required by that population are depleted, limiting further population growth and destabilizing the balance of the ecosystem. The correct answer, therefore, is (A).

72. The white feathers of the white-tailed ptarmigan are a survival advantage in a snowy environment since they provide camouflage. Camouflage is one example of an adaptation that increases the survival rates for organisms; ptarmigans with winter plumage that did not blend with the snow would not be as likely to survive to reproduce; the genes for those colors would then be eliminated from the gene pool. Traits that provide a survival advantage are adaptations, and they become common due to natural selection. Therefore, the correct answer is (D).

73. This question asks for knowledge of the solar system. As Earth rotates on its axis, a given location on the planet will alternate between daytime and night as that location will first face the Sun and then face away from the Sun. It is Earth's rotation that causes the cycle of daylight and night. The correct answer, therefore, is (C).

74. This question requires knowledge of the benefits of forests to society. Among the benefits of preserving forests is the preservation of plants, which are a common source of many of our current drugs. Pharmaceutical companies study the compounds extracted from plants to determine whether they have potential medical applications. The correct answer is (A).

75. This question requires an understanding of the processes that have led to changes in species over time. Although both colors of moths were present before the Industrial Revolution, the light-colored moths were more prevalent because their coloration provided an adaptive advantage. Light-colored moths were camouflaged on the existing light-colored surfaces and would be more apt to survive to reproduce. As tree bark and other surfaces became darker because of industrialization, the survival rate of dark-colored moths increased and that of light-colored moths decreased. There was natural selection in favor of the dark-colored moths. The correct answer, therefore, is (B).

76. This question requires familiarity with contributions made by major historical figures. The theory of natural selection was the work of Charles Darwin and refers to the idea that the best-suited organisms will live to reproduce, passing their advantageous traits, or adaptations, on to subsequent generations. Those individuals lacking these traits will not survive to reproduce. The correct answer, therefore, is (A).

77. This question requires the interpretation of graphical data. The largest uniformly shaded area on the graph, the dotted region, represents the source that contributed the greatest amount of carbon monoxide emissions. Comparing the dotted shading on the graph with the key, you can see that transportation, choice (C), is the correct answer.

78. This question asks you to draw conclusions based on the information presented in the stimulus. More cars would produce more carbon monoxide (CO), but newer cars emit less CO than older cars. These conditions have opposite effects on CO emissions, but if the relative magnitude of each is not known, neither is the net effect of these changes on CO emissions. Since the effect of all other sources of CO remains constant and the effect of the changes in automobile transportation cannot be determined, it is not possible to determine the relative amount of carbon monoxide emissions in 2003. The correct answer, therefore, is (D).

79. This question asks for an understanding of the basic properties of matter. By measuring the volume of water that is displaced by the stone when it is added to the beaker, Natasha is measuring the amount of space that is occupied by the stone, which is the definition of volume. The correct answer, therefore, is (B).

80. This question requires knowledge of the basic properties of matter. The density of an object is the ratio of its mass to its volume. The stone sinks in the water because it has a greater mass than the mass of an equal volume of water. Therefore, the density of the stone is greater than the density of the water. The correct answer is (C).

Chapter 7

Are You Ready? Last-Minute Tips

▶   ▶   ▶   ▶   ▶   ▶   ▶   ▶   ▶   ▶   ▶   ▶

Checklist

Complete this checklist to determine whether you're ready to take the test.

❏ Do you know the testing requirements for your field in the state(s) where you plan to practice?

❏ Have you followed all of the test registration procedures?

❏ Do you know the topics covered by the test?

❏ Have you reviewed any textbooks, class notes, and course readings related to the topics covered?

❏ Do you know how long the test will take and the number of questions it contains? Have you considered how you will pace your work?

❏ Are you familiar with the test directions and the types of questions in the test?

❏ Are you familiar with the recommended test-taking strategies and tips?

❏ Have you worked through the practice test questions at a pace similar to that of an actual test?

❏ If you are repeating a Praxis Series™ Assessment, have you analyzed your previous score report to determine areas where additional study and test preparation could be useful?

The Day of the Test

You should end your review a day or two before the actual test date. The day of the test you should

- be well rested

- take photo identification with you

- take a supply of well-sharpened #2 pencils (at least three) and a nonprogrammable calculator

- take your admission ticket, letter of authorization, mailgram or telegram with you

- eat before you take the test to keep your energy level up

- wear layered clothing; room temperature may vary

- be prepared to stand in line to check in or to wait while other test takers are being checked in

You can't control the testing situation, but you can control yourself. Stay calm. The supervisors are well trained and make every effort to provide uniform testing conditions, but don't let it bother you if the test doesn't start exactly on time. You will have the full amount of time once it does start.

Think of preparing for this test as training for an athletic event. Once you've trained, prepared, and rested, give it everything you've got. Good luck.

Appendix A
Study Plan Sheet

► ► ► ► ► ► ► ► ► ► ► ►

Study Plan Sheet

See Chapter 1 for suggestions on using this Study Plan Sheet.

STUDY PLAN						
Content covered on test	How well do I know the content?	What material do I have for studying this content?	What material do I need for studying this content?	Where could I find the materials I need?	Dates planned for study of content	Dates completed

Appendix B
For More Information

▶   ▶   ▶   ▶   ▶   ▶   ▶   ▶   ▶   ▶   ▶   ▶

Educational Testing Service offers additional information to assist you in preparing for the Praxis Series™ Assessments. *Tests at a Glance* booklets and the *Registration Bulletin* are both available without charge. You can also obtain more information from our Web site: http://www.ets.org/praxis/index.html.

General Inquiries

Phone: 800-772-9476 or 609-771-7395 (Monday-Friday, 8:00 A.M. to 7:45 P.M., Eastern time)
Fax: 609-771-7906

Extended Time

If you have a learning disability or if English is not your primary language, you can apply to be given more time to take your test. The *Registration Bulletin* tells you how you can qualify for extended time.

Disability Services

Phone: 866-387-8602 or 609-771-7780
Fax: 609-771-7906
TTY (for deaf or hard-of-hearing callers): 609-771-7714

Mailing Address

ETS – The Praxis Series
P.O. Box 6051
Princeton, NJ 08541-6051

Overnight Delivery Address

ETS – The Praxis Series
Distribution Center
225 Phillips Blvd.
P.O. Box 77435
Ewing, NJ 08628-7435